Gary Jones

Scandinavia

Contents

1

COPENHAGEN INTRODUCTION

Before heading out to Copenhagen, you should arm yourself with useful information. This book provides you with all the things you need to know about this beautiful city.

Here are a few things you can learn through this travel guide:

-Discover how this beautiful city came to be by exploring its history briefly

-Travel like a local by learning which public transportation to take at which time

-Learn about each neighborhood and what they have to offer

-Find out when the best time to pay Copenhagen a visit is

-Discover more about the city's rich history with our list of best museums

-Explore the art and culture of Copenhageners from their exquisite displays in the best art galleries

-Find out where to get the best coffee in the city

-Let the Copenhageners show you how to party with our list of best bars and nightclubs

-Book a superb accommodation at affordable prices with our list of budget friendly hotels

-Have a unique gastronomic experience like no other with Copenhagen's best restaurants

-Have an unforgettable experience doing special things that can only be done in Copenhagen

Also included is a sample 3-day itinerary to make your trip pleasant and organized.

Thanks again for downloading this book, I hope you enjoy it!

2

A Brief History of Copenhagen

A Brief History of Copenhagen

The biggest Scandinavian city and the capital of Denmark, Copen-hagen is a busy business hub and center for the arts and culture. The city offers plenty of entertainment options. It is also known as a culinary hotspot, offering a unique gastronomic experience.

Copenhagen was built!

Copenhagen was founded in 1167 by King Valdemar I's counsellor, Bishop Absalon. Valdemar the Great tasked Absalon to build the city in an effort to protect the trade. The first fortress was built on the isle of Slotsholmen. The original castle of Absalon has now become the foundation of the Christianborg Palace.

Because of its ideal location for harbor, Copenhagen rose from a simple fishing village to a respectable city in the 12th century. In 1443, Copenhagen became the Danish capital, replacing Roskilde.

The first King of Denmark was crowned in Copenhagen in 1449, King Christian I. He founded the first university in Denmark, the historical Copenhagen University.

The Reformation Era

In 1536, the Protestant Reformation came to Copenhagen and Denmark. With the initiative of King Christian III who ruled in 1503 to 1559, the Protestant movement was introduced in the country. It marked the reformation of the Danish Church. Today, 90 percent of Danes are members of the Evangelian-Lutheran Church.

The Architect of Copenhagen

From 1588 to 1648, a ruler known as the great builder and architect of Copenhagen by the name of King Christian IV reigned. During his reign, plenty of remarkable projects and building were constructed. The first and now the world's oldest amusement park, the Bakken, was built during his time. The Old Citadel, which protected the city against England in the Battle of Copenhagen in 1807, was also built under King Christian IV's rule. Other notable projects that still stand today include the Round Tower built in 1642, the Old Stock Exchange built in 1620 and the Rosenborg Castle in 1634.

When King Christian IV died at the age of 70 in 1648, King Frederik III was crowned. He continued the works of his predecessor and went on to build the Royal Library. The Royal Danish Guards were also

6

established under his rule.

Copenhagen in the 18th Century

The economy and trade continued to grow in the 18th century. Unfortunately, Copenhagen witnessed and suffered plenty of misfortunes during this time. In 1711, the Bubonic plague wiped out close to a third of the population. In 1728, fires ruined and heavily damaged the city. The Copenhageners were quick to recover, however. In 1737, reconstruction and rebuilding of the city was completed.

The first newspaper of Copenhagen, the Royal Danish Theatre, the first free hospital and the Royal Danish Porcelain factory were all established. It would seem that Copenhagen was back on its feet. Unfortunately, Copenhagen was attacked by the British with their heavy bombs. The city suffered in casualties and destruction from 1801 to 1807.

The spirit of the Danish people was rekindled in 1808. The year marked the tradition of Christmas celebration in the city. it also paved the way to unite the Danish Christian culture.

Denmark went bankrupt in 1813. The economy eventually recovered over the years and still going strong today as evident in modern Copenhagen.

3

Transport and Safety

Getting Into The City

If you are flying into Copenhagen, you will arrive at Copenhagen Airport, Kastrup. You will have many transport options to get into the city. You can get into the city by subway, train, bus or taxi.

Phone: +45 32 31 32 31 (airport)
Airport Website
https://www.cph.dk/en/
Airport Map
https://goo.gl/maps/zB88rc4WqQw

Getting around Copenhagen is easy and simple. That's because you can access the trains, Metro, buses and waterbuses using the same ticket. The public transport is also reliable and punctual. Here is a list of the transports that can take you around the city.

Copenhagen Card

A good option for cheap travel is the Copenhagen Card that will give you many benefits including the following:

-Free admission to 74 museums and attractions.
-Free transport by train, bus, harbour bus and Subway in the entire Copenhagen Region – also from and to the airport.
-Discounts on car hire, restaurants and sights.
Copenhagen Card Website
http://www.copenhagencard.com/whats-included

By Bus

Copenhagen's primary buses are called A-buses. They will take you around the city center. They are open to serve the public at all hours. You can cut your travel time by taking the S-buses because they have fewer stops. Rush hour is between 7 and 9 in the morning and 3:30 to 5:30 in the afternoon.

Bus Website
http://www.dsb.dk/en

By Metro

Copenhagen's Metro is available 24/7.
Metro Website
http://www.dsb.dk/en

By Train

There are different lines depending on the route. The S-trains are open from 5am to 12:30 at night. Lines A, B, C and E run every 10 minutes while lines H and Bx every 20 minutes. Line F runs every 4 minutes.

If you want a slow tour of the city, you can also take a boat ride by the canal.

Train Website
http://www.dsb.dk/en

Bicycles

When in Copenhagen you should rent a bike and explore the city.The people of Copenhagen are known for their love of riding bikes. It is biking heaven in Copenhagen.The city has over 390 kilometers of designated bike lanes.

Bicycles Rental Website
http://copenhagenbicycles.dk/rent/
Bicycles Rental Map
https://goo.gl/maps/XVVUkARAZY62

Safety in Copenhagen

This is generally a safe city. However, just like other busy cities, you need to take precautions during your stay.

Be wary of pickpockets especially around the central station. Thieves also abound in the busy pedestrian street of Strøget and around the City Hall Square. Some tourists have been scammed by individuals posing as police officers. If you are approached by a police officer, ask for legitimate identification. The Copenhagen police will not ask you to pay fines on the spot for breaking a law.

The Copenhagen police can be contacted at 114. During emergency situations, call 112.

4

Areas of Copenhagen

Copenhagen has plenty of interesting sights to see and things to experience. The following are the different areas in the city and the best they could offer to tourists.

Tivoli Gardens

Built in 1843, Tivoli Gardens is found in the south of Rådhuspladsen. These amusement gardens have a fantastic lineup of theaters, dance halls, restaurants and beer gardens. This is where you will see exotic flowers. Tivoli has about 160,000 of them. It is beautifully adorned with 110,000 electric lights. It is also surrounded by beautiful lakes that further contribute to its serene and fairy tale atmosphere. The Tivoli Gardens is one of the many reasons why thousands of tourists visit Copenhagen each year.

In addition to the lush gardens and charming architecture, Tivoli also offers magical rides. Among the most famous is the Vertigo which is an thrilling ride that turns upside down at a speed of 100 km/h. It was actually named Europe's Best Ride in 2014. Another popular ride is the wooden Roller Coaster built in 1914. It's an old school roller coaster with a brakeman on board that mans each train.

The Tivoli Gardens is most crowded during the summer but the amusement park also holds special events throughout the year. It is highly recommended whether you are travelling with your kids or on a romantic vacation.

Tivoli Gardens Website
https://www.tivoli.dk/en/
Tivoli Gardens Map
https://goo.gl/maps/SMr7M6zGjg22

Strøget

Strøget consists of 5 interconnected streets: Østergade, Amager-torv, Villelskaftet, Nygade and Frederiksberggade. This is where you will find two of Copenhagen's busiest plazas, the Kongens Nytorv and the Rådhuspladsen. Also found in this area are two smaller squares which are equally spectacular, the Nytorv and Gammeltorv. These squares come alive during the summer with plenty of outdoor seating outside its marvelous lineup of restaurants.

Strøget Map
https://goo.gl/maps/vMbBCqi3hwE2

Nyhavn or Kongens Nytorv

Nyhavn means "New Harbor." Originally built in 1670, Nyhavn provided shelter for sailors during storms. It was also a place here sailors used to stop by for cheap drinks, tattoos and other kinds of diversions. Today, some of the antique fishing boats are still here which gives the area an old fashion charm. It has an exciting lineup of restaurants. In fact, it houses most of Copenhagen's best restaurants.

There are outdoor terraces as well which are usually filled on holidays when the Danes like to chatter

and drink hard. Above the Nyhavn canal, the King's New Market or Kongens Nytorv is found where the Royal Theater and the deluxe Hotel d'Angleterre are located.

Nyhavn or Kongens Nytorv Map
https://goo.gl/maps/UQ3HRCEmfw62

Indre By

Found at the heart of Copenhagen, Indre By is a beautiful Old Town. The neighborhood once consisted of monasteries, beautiful squares and a maze of alley ways and streets. Today, you will find charming buildings that links to the university. The Round Tower or Rundetårn and the Cathedral of Copenhagen or Vor Frue Kirke can be found in this area.

Indre By Map
https://goo.gl/maps/7NVrRWieuV42

Slotsholmen

In this side of Copenhagen lies the Christiansborg Palace which was where the first fortress was built by Bishop Absalon in 1167. Today, this island is home to the Thorvaldsen's Museum, the Danish parliament, the Royal Library, the Royal Museum and the Theatre Museum. You will also find the 17th-century Børsen or stock exchange here. You can get here by taking the bridge that links Indre By to this neighborhood.

Slotsholmen Map
https://goo.gl/maps/aXup7MA6MPS2

Christianshavn

Originally built according to the Dutch Renaissance style mainly for workers of the shipbuilding industry, this "new town" of the 1500's has seen many changes. Today, it is most popular for its attractions including the Vors Frelsers Kirke and the Danish Film Museum. The spire of the church provides a steep climb where visitors can marvel at the beautiful panoramic view of the city.

This area also houses the free city of Christiana which used serve as barracks for soldiers and home to the youth and homeless people. Today, restaurants and craft shops can be found near Christiana in the Prinsessegade area. The prices of food and goods here are quite cheap simply because the residents do not want to pay 25% sales tax.

Christianshavn Map
https://goo.gl/maps/aRNqScGkV332

Vesterbro

What used to be a slum for prostitutes and junkies has now become a place where Copenhagen's hippest bars, cafes and ethnic restaurants are found. People come here to party and experience cultural diversity. Although Vesterbro does not have famous museums and monuments, it does have plenty of other things to offer like food markets, ethnic gift shops and even sex shops.

Vesterbro Map
https://goo.gl/maps/WfhVXac99xT2

Nørrebro

Found right next to Vesterbro is Nørrebro where immigrants abound. This neighborhood is overflowing with ethnic restaurants and artisan shops, mostly Pakistani and Turkish. There are antique shops everywhere too especially along Ravnsborgade.

Nørrebro also houses the Assistens Kirkegård, Copenhagen's historic cemetery where the remains of Søren Kierkegaard and Hans Christian Andersen lay rest. Nørrebro also has an exciting night scene. The best nightlife hotspots in the city are found in

Blågårdsgade and Sankt Hans Torv.

Nørrebro Map
https://goo.gl/maps/LKVu8z5EWc62

Frederiksberg

This is both a business and residential district. Its focal point is the Frederiksberg Palace with a rich Italian style and a charming ocher facade. The surrounding area is a park called the Frederiksberg Have. To the west is the Zoologisk Have, one of Europe's largest zoos.

Frederiksberg Map
https://goo.gl/maps/vQbJ2kLV6t82

Dragør

This 16th century fishing village is now a favorite leisure spot in Copenhagen. Dragør boasts of national landmarks including the 65 old red-roofed houses and cobblestone streets. It is a superb representation of 18th-century Danish village.

Dragør Map
https://goo.gl/maps/hgvFUAU5QWt

5

So when is the best time to visit Copenhagen?

The weather is loveliest during the summer, that's between May and September. During the warm months, the streets are alive, the cafés and restaurants set up outdoor seating where guests can enjoy the lovely breeze. The summer months also have plenty to offer when it comes to festivals and other events.

When October comes, the festivals are over and Copenhagen prepares for the harsh winter. In December, the mood becomes festive and preparations are made for the holiday celebrations.

It is best to visit Copenhagen between June and August. Among the key events these times of the year include the Copenhagen Jazz Festival, Roskilde Festival and the Little Mermaid's Birthday. The downside is your trip will be a little more expensive. Because of the heavy influx of tourists, hotel accommodations and other expenses are higher.

From September to November, the weather becomes a little more frigid. The upside is that it is much less expensive to travel and stay at Copenhagen during the autumn. Plus, there are a few events you can still join and enjoy during your stay including the Copenhagen Blues Festival in September and Copenhagen Night of Culture in October.

March and May mark the spring time. The spring weather in Copenhagen is not as lovely as the summer. It is friendly and tolerable nevertheless. The best news is there are fewer crowds. Airfare and accommodations are also much lower. Tivoli Gardens is open by this time of the year. Notable Spring events include the Copenhagen Puppet Festival, the Copenhagen Beer Festival and the Copenhagen Carnival.

If your vacation budget allows it, you might as well go during the summer. Otherwise, you can go in spring or autumn.

6

The Best Museums in the City

The city of Copenhagen has many stories to tell. From the ancient palaces and castles to the narrow and cobblestone streets, everything speaks of its rich history. Learn more about the city from the Stone Age to the 20th century through the following best museums Copenhagen has to offer.

The National Museum

Housed in The Prince's Palace, the National Museum in itself along with its ornate pieces of furniture and elegant halls are part of rich history. Among the things that can be seen here are exhibitions of Danish history from the Stone Age to the Viking age to the middle ages to the Renaissance and Modern ages. Other notable things to see include the extensive ethnographical collection from coins to medals and toys.

The Danish antiquity that feature national treasures including the archeological discoveries that date back to the Viking Age, the Bronze Age Egtved Girl and the Sun Chariot, which is more than 3,000 years old. The remains of the Huldremose Woman from the first decade of the first century are also on display in this museum. Kids can have fun admiring history through the Children's Museum. There are English self-guided tours as well. The museum is open from Tuesdays to Sundays at 10am to 5am on February to December. Admission is free.

Address: Prince's Mansion, Ny Vestergade 10, 1471
The National Museum Website
http://en.natmus.dk/
The National Museum Map
https://goo.gl/maps/nWTKVVrYq3M2

The Museum of National History

The Frederiksborg Castle was burned down to the ground in 1859. It was rebuilt and restored as a museum in 1878. Also known as the Frederiksborg Museum, the National Historic Museum features historical paintings, portraits, furniture and other art works that speak of Denmark's history from the introduction of Christianity to the modern era.

You can visit this museum from Monday to Sundays between 10am to 5pm on April to October and between 11am to 3pm on November to March. The admission fee for adults is 75.00 DKK. Children from 6 to 15 years old are admitted for 20.00 DKK.

Address: 3400 Hillerød
The Museum of National History Website
http://www.dnm.dk/dk/index.htm
The Museum of National History Map
https://goo.gl/maps/MgMMdxsj2332

The Royal Danish Naval Museum

If you're interested in naval history, this is a must-see museum. The Royal Danish Naval Museum boasts of an extensive historic naval model collection including submarine interiors, uniforms, nautical instruments, marine paintings, ship decorations and naval artillery. It is a thrilling experience that gives you the opportunity to get up close and personal to more than 400 ship models on display that represent the shipbuilding development that has occurred over the past 300 years.

Children can have an exciting tour as they are given the opportunity to board a reconstruction of the Danish warship. Admission is free. The museum is open from Tuesday to Sunday between 12nn to 4pm on May to December.

Address: Overgaden Oven Vandet 58, 1415
The Royal Danish Naval Museum Website
http://natmus.dk/museerne/orlogsmuseet/
The Royal Danish Naval Museum Map
https://goo.gl/maps/sQzLWGczz6u

Thorvaldsen's Museum

Bertel Thorvaldsen, a renowned Danish sculptor in the 1800s donated his art collection to Copenhagen, his native city. His large collection is housed in one of Copenhagen's finest buildings designed by M.B. Bindesbøll and built from 1839 to 1848. This museum is home to Thorvaldsen's sculpture masterpieces. His antique and painting collections are also on display.

The museum is open from Tuesdays to Sundays from 10am to 5pm on January to December. Admission fee for adults is 40.00 DKK.

Admission for visitors below 18 years of age is free.

Address:Bertel Thorvaldsens Plads 2, 1213
Thorvaldsen's Museum Website
http://www.thorvaldsensmuseum.dk/en
Thorvaldsen's Museum Map
https://goo.gl/maps/A4VZxJ9wbRy

The Workers' Museum

Are you curious about how average Copenhageners lived in the 50's? This museum shows you just how. The Workers' Museum recounts stories of working class families including that of the Sørensen family. Visitors get the chance to taste what was popular in those days including the kiksekage, a rich cracker cake and the wartime coffee substitute. The museum has a dedicated area for 20th century homes and shops called the People's Century Lane.

The museum is open every day between 10am and 4pm. Admission for adults is 65.00 DKK. Admission is free for visitors under the age of 18 years.

Address:Rømersgade 22, 1362
The Workers' Museum Website
http://www.arbejdermuseet.dk/
The Workers' Museum Map
https://goo.gl/maps/MyUYoLa9Nzn

7

The Best Art Galleries

Along with its rich history, Copenhagen is also a haven for the arts. If you are a fan of art, you can explore the Danish and international art scene from the Golden Age to the contemporary era in these beautiful galleries.

The National Gallery of Denmark

This is the largest art museum in Denmark featuring exquisite art from Danish and other artists from the past 700 years. There are Renaissance classics as well as modern and contemporary art. The most popular is the beautiful art collection from the Danish Golden Age. The gallery boasts of Matisse's best collections.

The National Gallery of Denmark holds several art-based events throughout the year where visitors can join in art talks and music while enjoying food and drinks. The Royal Cast Collection which features more than 2000 plaster sculptures representing over 4000 years of history about Christian tales and pagan gods is also a part of the gallery.

The gallery offers guided tours and workshop activities. Children and families can join in the drawing room and exhibitions to explore their inner creativity.

The museum is open on Tuesdays, Thursdays to Sundays from 10am to 5pm on January to December. They are also open on Wednesdays between 10am and 8pm. Admission is free on the permanent exhibitions. Adult admission fee for special exhibitions is at 110.00 DKK and 85.00 DKK for young adults.

Address:Sølvgade 48-50, 1307
The National Gallery of Denmark Website
http://www.smk.dk/en/
The National Gallery of Denmark Map
https://goo.gl/maps/ob3SD7SiKMv

The Hirschsprung Collection

19th and early 20th century Danish art is represented well in this gallery. The Hirschsprung Collection features art works from the Danish Golden Age to the Skagen and all the way to Modern Breakthrough. Masterpieces from Hammershøi, Krøyer, Købke and Eckersberg are on display.

The beautiful collection is housed in a stunning neo-classical style building of special importance located in central Copenhagen. A tobacco manufacturer by the name of Heinrich Hirschsprung donated his personal art collection in 1902 to the Danish state. The gallery is designed and built around his collection where it is now enjoyed by the Danes and visitors from all over the world.

The gallery is open from Tuesdays to Sundays between 11am to 4pm from November to December. Admission fee for adults is at 75.00 DKK and free for visitors under 18 years old. On Wednesdays, entrance is free for everyone.

Address:Stockholmsgade 20, 2100

The Hirschsprung Collection Website
http://www.hirschsprung.dk/default.aspx
The Hirschsprung Collection Map
https://goo.gl/maps/P9vgPGg7ARm

Glyptoteket

Founded by the renowned brewer, Carl Jacobsen in 1888, Glyp-toteket consists of two departments: the ancient and modern art. The gallery has an extensive display of exquisite artwork, and the architectural surroundings is just as stunning.

In the Department of Antiquities, visitors will find fine collections of artworks from Egyptians, Greeks, Etruscans and Romans. It will take you to 3500 years of history and art.

The Modern Department, on the other hand, features sculptures and paintings from the 19th to 20th centuries from Danish and French artists. Among the things that Glyptoteket boasts of are the 35 sculptures by Rodin, Degas' complete series of bronzes, 40+ works by Gauguin along with the finest works from the Denmark's Golden Age and French Impressionism. Glyptoteket also holds special exhibitions to enhance the public's art experience.

The gallery is open on Tuesdays, Wednesdays and Friday to Sundays between 11am and 6pm from March to December. They are also open on Thursdays from 11am to 10pm. The admission fee for adults is 95.00 DKK and free for visitors under 18 years old.

Address:Dantes Plads 7, 1556
Glyptoteket Website
http://www.glyptoteket.com/
Glyptoteket Map
https://goo.gl/maps/mrYLcySt8632

Kunsthal Charlottenborg

One of Europe's largest contemporary art spaces, Kunsthal Charlottenborg has a strong international focus. It has plenty of events and exhibitions with screenings, talks and performances all in an effort to reach a wider range of audiences. The art space mounts 3 seasons annually. It is known in Copenhagen as a true champion of contemporary art.

The gallery is open on Wednesdays between 11am and 8pm on May to December. It also opens from Tuesdays to Sundays 11am to 5pm throughout the months of May. Admission fee for adults us 60.00 DKK and free for visitors below 16 years old.

Address:Nyhavn 2, 1051
Kunsthal Charlottenborg Website
http://www.charlottenborg.dk/forside?lang=eng
Kunsthal Charlottenborg Map
https://goo.gl/maps/CBzCfYbPnSM2

Den Frie Centre of Contemporary Art

The gallery has a long standing tradition of supporting contemporary art and architecture. Houses in a wooden building designed by J.F. Willumsen and founded in 1898, Den Frie prides itself as a house of artists, envisioning the art of the future.

The gallery is open on Tuesdays, Wednesdays, and Friday to Sundays between 12nn and 6pm from January to December. It also opens on Thursdays from 12nn to 9pm. The admission fee for adults is 60.00 DKK and free for visitors below 12 years old.

Address:Oslo Pl. 1, 2100

Den Frie Centre of Contemporary Art Website
http://en.denfrie.dk/
Den Frie Centre of Contemporary Art Map
https://goo.gl/maps/kNAriJbuyz12

8

The Best Coffee Shops in Copenhagen

Copenhagen does not fall short when it comes to great quality coffee. Because of the cold weather, the Copenhageners appreciate excellent coffee and there are plenty of shops that serve a good cup around the city. Here are a couple of coffee shops you should try while you're in the city.

Kent Kaffe Laboratorium

Located in the neighborhood of Indre By along Nørre Farimagsgade, Kent Kaffe Laboratorium offers a unique experience for coffee lovers. They are most known for their classics as well as their impressively advanced brewing methods. The coffee beans they use are 100 percent organic, imported from different parts of the world.

As the name suggests, the interior is laboratory inspired. Customers are encouraged to experiment with their coffee. You can even have yours in a flask brewed over a bunsen burner. Kent Kaffe Laboratorium serves a wide range of breads and cakes including the organic face sandwich the Copenhageners call smørrebrød.

This coffee shop is open from Monday to Friday between 9am and 5:30pm. It also opens on Saturdays from 11am to 5pm and on Sundays from 12nn to 5pm.

Address: Nørre Farimagsgade 70, 1364
Kent Kaffe Laboratorium Website
http://www.kentkaffelaboratorium.com/
Kent Kaffe Laboratorium Map
https://goo.gl/maps/8DyqHryepeB2

The Coffee Collective, Jægersborggade

The Coffee Collective is more than just a coffee shop. They are making a great effort to provide extraordinary coffee experience by paying much attention to the coffee making process. In cooperation with farmers, The Coffee Collective aims to develop a more sustainable way of producing and improving coffee quality. You will experience the difference when you taste their great coffee.

The coffee shop is open to serve great coffee on Mondays to Fridays from 7am to 7pm on July to December. They are also open on the weekends from 8am to 7pm.

At Jægersborggade, the atmosphere is relaxing and the baristas are welcoming. The Coffee Collective also has to other shops located in Gothåbsvej and Torvehallerne.

Address: Jægersborggade 10, 2200
The Coffee Collective, Jægersborggade Website
http://coffeecollective.dk/
The Coffee Collective, Jægersborggade Map
https://goo.gl/maps/wVFWNoqCij92

Coffee First

Used to be Estate Coffee, Coffee First is a rather small coffee shop located across the street from the lakes and the Planetarium. People come here for a taste of their unbeatable estate coffee. Another must try from this place are their delicious chocolate desserts that hail from Strangas. They also serve breakfast plates at DKK 79.

This coffee shop located along Gammel Kongevej is open on weekdays of March to December between 7:30am and 8pm. On weekends, they are open from 10am to 8pm.

Address: Gammel Kongevej 1, 1610
Coffee First Website
https://sites.google.com/site/wwwcoffeefirstdk/
Coffee First Map
https://goo.gl/maps/TCPftDWEcpN2

Parterre

Found in the maritime Christianshavn district, Parterre is a newly established coffee shop that has quickly earned an excellent reputation. This basement coffee has a rustic feel to it but with the lights and the beautiful decorations, the shop has a unique appeal. In fact, customers like to take pictures in the café.

This coffee shop in Indre By along Ovengaden Oven Vandet serves coffee on weekdays between 7am and 6pm. They are also open on weekends from 9am to 6pm. They are open to serve throughout the year.

More than the nice interior however, people stop by the Parterre for the excellent coffee that comes from the Koppi, a Swedish roaster. For a good cup of coffee, the prices at Parterre are very reasonable. A coffee cup will only cost you between 26.00 and 36.00 DKK

Breakfast and lunch plates are also available. You can also have some delicious cake slices to enjoy with your coffee.

Address: Overgaden Oven Vandet 90, 1415
Parterre Website
https://goo.gl/hG1hFy
Parterre Map
https://goo.gl/maps/owbxfNBWmg32

Kafferiet

If you want variety, you can head to the Kafferiet at Esplanaden. They serve 15 different types of coffee. They also offer iced coffee, smoothies, tea, sandwiches, muffins and croissants. You can order coffee to go and stroll around the Citadel too. Or you can buy five different kinds of coffee beans from them so you can make some at home.

Found along Esplanaden, Kafferiet serves coffee on weekdays from 7:30am to 6pm and on weekends from 10am to 6pm all year round.

Address: Esplanaden 44, 1263
Kafferiet Website
https://goo.gl/exc1lO
Kafferiet Map
https://goo.gl/maps/VnNbzSeiaJJ2

Risteriet, Studiestræde

Located along the lively street of Studiestræde, Risteriet offers a great selection of coffee beans. You can buy aromatic beans from them or some coffee equipment. They also sell green coffee beans if you fancy roasting some yourself.

If you don't want to go through all the trouble of making coffee for yourself, you can have a cup at Risteriet and enjoy it from the outside seating where you can bask at a nice view of the streets. Risteriet has another shop located at the Vesterbro neighborhood along Halmtorvet.

Located in the neighborhood of Indre By, Risteriet is open on weekends from 8am to 6pm, on Saturdays from 10am to 5pm and on Sundays from 10am to 3pm throughout the year.

Address: Studiestræde 36, 1455
Risteriet, Studiestræde Website
http://www.risteriet.dk/
Risteriet, Studiestræde Map
https://goo.gl/maps/Pm1ezdZxf692

Original Coffee

Nothing beats a good coffee taht you can enjoy around a cosy atmosphere. That is exactly what the Original Coffee offers. They serve high quality coffee with a great variety. The beans are locally roasted. They also offer Irish Coffees as well as sandwiches and decadent cakes that come from an organic bakery.

A minimalistic style interior, Original Coffee provides a safe haven for their customers where they can enjoy their coffee in a stress-free environment. Original Coffee has three more shops located at Bredgade, Strandvejen and Trianglen. The shop at Nordre Frihavnsgade in Trianglen has a great view of the lake. It was in fact, voted as the best coffee shop in Copenhagen of 2013.

Address: Østergade 52, 1001
Original Coffee
https://www.facebook.com/originalcoffee/
Original Coffee
https://goo.gl/maps/oQkTBcHRukF2

Café Glyptoteket

Glyptoteket is not only a place of art. It is also a place for a relaxing cup of coffee. Another beautiful sight at the art museum is the beautiful winter garden where Café Glyptoteket is found. The café serves coffee, sumptuous cakes and homemade Danish lunch dishes. The owners use sustainable and organic ingredients. Relax with a cup of coffee at hand as you enjoy every sip surrounded by exotic flowers, plants and palm trees.

Café Glyptoteket is open from Tuesdays to Sundays between 11am and 5pm throughout December. Prices of dishes range between DKK 95 and DKK 200.

<u>Address:</u> Dantes Plads 7, 1556
Café Glyptoteket Website
http://www.glyptoteket.dk/besoeg/cafe
Café Glyptoteket Map
https://goo.gl/maps/jK9Usgaa5fz

9

The Best Bars and Night Clubs

Copenhageners know how to have a great time. It shows with their excellent line up of bars and clubs that guarantees a night of fun. If you like to party or simply have a drink or two before heading to your hotel, check out these cool spots in Copenhagen.

WarPigs

Serving 22 quality taps, WarPigs is very well known for providing an extraordinary beer experience. Expect nothing less from this brew-pub established by two big names in the brewery scene, American brewery 3 Floyds and Danish brewer Mikkeller. They have an on-site brewery. They do not only offer freshly made craft beer, WarPigs also serve authentic Texas barbecue.

Address: Flæsketorvet 25, 1117 København K
Phone: +45 4348 4848
WarPigs Website
http://warpigs.dk/
WarPigs Map
https://goo.gl/maps/uiRJt1UY2Zv

Mikkeler Bar

Established by no other than the world famous brewer Mikkel Borg Bjergsø in 2007, Mikkeler Bar is known for offering 10 taps from Mikkeler itself and 5 others from world's best breweries. They also serve the best snacks and cheese. Specialized bottled selections are also available.

The bar is open to serve on Mondays to Wednesdays and Sundays from 1pm to 1am, on Thursdays to Fridays from 1pm to 2am and on Saturdays between 12nn and 2am on October to December. Check out Mikkeler and Friends at Copenhagen's Nørrebro area too.

Address: Victoriagade 8 B-C, 1655 København V
Phone: +45 33310415
Mikkeler Website
http://mikkeller.dk/location/mikkeller-bar-aarhus/
Mikkeler Map
https://goo.gl/maps/GrMgwSgA500

1105

Known as a trendy bar for the 30-something, 1105 serves magical potions in the form of topnotch cocktails. The atmosphere is modern and chic. The bar also serves modern shakes and classic cocktails. A must-try is the Copenhagen cocktail, an original creation of 1105's cocktail tender, Gromit.

The cocktail bar is open on Fridays from 4pm to 2am, on Wednesdays, Thursdays and Saturdays between 8pm and 2am all year round.

Address: Kristen Bernikows Gade 4, 1105 København K
Phone: +45 3393 1105
1105 Website
http://www.1105.dk/
1105 Map
https://goo.gl/maps/XuWWixvyaot

HIVE

An exclusive club found near Gammeltorv, Hive always has something exciting in store for party hungry peeps. On Fridays, Hive caters to an energetic audience. The club ensures the music doesn't stop with their excellent DJ lineup. On Saturdays, Hive completely transforms itself playing mixes from the 1300s complete with dungeons along with 3-dimensional visuals.

The club is only open on Fridays and Saturdays between 11pm and 5am from January to December. If you happen to check them out though, you are guaranteed to have a fun, unforgettable evening.

Address: Skindergade 45-47, 1159 København K
Phone: +45 2845 7467
HIVE Website
https://goo.gl/oXPjms

HIVE Map
https://goo.gl/maps/wcf63CN1en92

Culture Box

If you are a huge fan of electronic music, Culture Box is the place to be. This is one of Denmark's most prominent nightclubs. It is known for bringing together underground local artists and also an impressive line-up of international artists. The club consists of three compartments.

The White Box is designed as a pre-clubbing bar. The Red Box provides a more intimate atmosphere located in the lower floor and the Black Box is built with a massive sound system where guests can check out some of the biggest names in the music scene.

Culture Box plays a mix of electronica, house, techno and bass music. They are open on Fridays and Saturdays from 11pm onwards throughout the year. The admission fee ranges between 50.00 DKK and 100.00 DKK.

Address: Kronprinsessegade 54 St., 1306 København K
Phone: +45 3332 5050
Culture Box Website
http://www.culture-box.com/
Culture Box Map
https://goo.gl/maps/44GJSmq8jq32

10

Top 4 Affordable Hotels

You don't have to spend a lot on accommodation. There are plenty of excellent but inexpensive hotels in Copenhagen. These 4 are at the top of the list.

Wake Up Copenhagen

Planted in a central location, Wake Up is found in the south side of Copenhagen's main train station. It's not the quietest. The surrounding is slightly industrial. Although it's a budget hotel, its compact rooms are impressively designed according to slick Scandinavian style complete with modern amenities. The rate for standard double rooms starts at £60. If you can spare extra £25-35 a night, you can get a room on the top floor that gives you a stunning view of the city.

Address: Carsten Niebuhrs Gade 11, 1577
Phone:+45 4480 0000
Wake Up Copenhagen Website
https://www.wakeupcopenhagen.com/#/search
Wake Up Copenhagen Map
https://goo.gl/maps/i1UMxwPxrBL2

Hotel Sct Thomas

There's an area in Copenhagen fondly called small Paris. It's in Værndedamsvej which is a street found in between Frederiksberg and Vesterbro. Værndedamsvej is a nice area in Copenhagen because it has an array of food shops, bars, and restaurants. The Hotel of Sct Thomas is located in a residential area, a stone throw away from Copenhagen's culinary hotspot, parks and the hip bars of Vesterbro.

Although the rooms are rather small, they are tastefully decorated. Being in a residential area, the hotel guarantees its guests a peaceful night's sleep. The rate of their double rooms starts at £78.

Address: Frederiksberg Alle 7, 1621
Phone:+45 3321 6464

Hotel Sct Thomas Website
http://www.hotelsctthomas.dk/
Hotel Sct Thomas Map
https://goo.gl/maps/uLbP3kifEJA2

Tivoli Hotel

This is a newly established hotel meant to accommodate the visitors of the theme park, Tivoli Gardens. The hotel may not share the same historical charm that the 168-year old theme park boasts of but Tivoli Hotel does feature some classic elements borrowed from the park.

Aside from the basic modern amenities, Tivoli Hotel offers various entertainment options for their guests. They have a pool and both indoor and outdoor play area which makes the hotel ideal for families. They have special deals for vacationing families too. The rate for double rooms starts at £110 which already includes entry fee to the Tivoli Gardens.

Address: Arni Magnussons Gade 2, 1577
Phone:+45 4487 0000
Tivoli Hotel Website
http://www.tivolihotel.dk/
Tivoli Hotel Map
https://goo.gl/maps/PsyfNxjaC272

Ibsens Hotel

Found near the shopping street of Nansensgade, Ibsens has a charming location. It is sandwiched between the lakes that surround the city center and the downtown area. It is also a short walk away from the Nørreport train station which has routes going northbound the coastline that leads to Louisiana art museum and a connection to Sweden as well.

The hotel has a vintage feel to it. The design is very much inspired by local art and fashion. In addition to its charming and convenient location, Ibsens is quite affordable as well. The double rooms start at £100.

Address: Vendersgade 23, 1363
Phone:+45 3313 1913
Ibsens Hotel Website
http://www.arthurhotels.dk/ibsens-hotel/
Ibsens Hotel Map
https://goo.gl/maps/GMYxrdMJeZA2

11

Restaurants

Copenhagen attracts thousands of visitors from all over the world each year not only for their charming streets, lively events and rich art and history. Copenhagen is also known as a culinary hotspot. Do not miss out a unique gastronomic experience during your trip. Check out these delightful restaurants.

Madklubben Vesterbro

Found in the hip Vesterbro area, Madklubben has a wide range of menu. This restaurant is hard to miss because of its unique facade that looks like a transistor radio. They serve everything here from risotto to steak. They have classic Danish cuisines and international dishes. Customers can even put together their own menu. One-course meal is priced around DKK 100. Two-course meals are at DKK 150, three-course meals are at DKK 200 and four-course meals are at DKK 250.

Madklubben is known all over Copenhagen as a mid-budget restaurant with an intimate atmosphere that serves quality food. The restaurant is open daily between 5:30pm and 12mn on October to December.

Address: Vesterbrogade 62, 1620 København V
Phone: +45 3841 4143
Madklubben Vesterbro Website
http://madklubben.dk/en/
Madklubben Vesterbro Map
https://goo.gl/maps/UpkqwHMT4pG2

Geist

Danish celebrities rave about this cool restaurant. Owned by Chef Bo Bech, Geist serves tasty and well composed dishes. The most recommended from the menu is the mashed potato with brown stone crab and salted butter. Guests can also create their own menu by choosing two or three savory dishes paired with a sweet dish.

Geist looks like a high end restaurant but it is not as expensive as one might think. A dish can cost around DKK 81 to DKK 237. After the meal, have some coffee and sweet cotton candy. And after a sumptuous dinner, walk by the water at Nyhavn or take a boat tour.

Address: Kongens nytorv 8, 1050 København K
Phone: +45 33 13 37 13
Geist Website
http://restaurantgeist.dk/en/
Geist Map
https://goo.gl/maps/Mi1E8MVnLzp

Marv & Ben

Found along the charming medieval cobblestone street of Snare-gade, Marv & Ben is classified as a Bib Gourmand restaurant but prides itself as a gastro pub. They serve modern Danish cuisine. Their ingredients are fresh and local. In fact, the restaurant has its own garden. There are no complications in their menu. The dishes are unpretentious but ultimately flavorful.

Marv & Ben's menu changes from season to season to ensure optimum freshness in their ingredients. They are open on Tuesdays to Saturdays between 6pm and 12mn all year round. The price for two-course meals starts at DKK 325.

Address: Snaregade 4, 1205 København K
Phone: +45 3391 0191
Marv & Ben Website

http://cargocollective.com/marvogben
Marv & Ben Map
https://goo.gl/maps/6oN1UeBhyuT2

Cofoco Restaurant

This popular restaurant is found at the Vesterbro district. Cofoco stands for Copenhagen Food Consulting. Restaurant Cofoco is a favorite among menu because of their quality food offered at reasonable prices. The interior is designed according to contemporary style. Their trendy seating arrangements are quite comfortable. The price for their four-course meals is around DKK 275. The restaurant is open daily between 5:30pm and 12mn from October to December.

Address: Abel Cathrines Gade 7, 1650 København V
Phone: +45 3313 6060
Cofoco Restaurant Website
http://cofoco.dk/
Cofoco Restaurant Map
https://goo.gl/maps/6zk9mjn156w

Höst

Part of the Cofoco restaurant chain, Höst is found in the Nansensgade area near the lakes. The restaurant serves fine Nordic food at affordable prices. Their top rated dishes include the beef, lobster and Danish cheese hailed from the North Sea Coast.

The charming rooms are beautifully decorated in raw style. They use zinc, concrete, granite and recycled wood for the furnishings. Their benches and chairs are adorned with lambskin and plaids. Three-course meals start at DKK 295. Höst is open daily between 5:30pm and 12mn from October to December.

<u>Address:</u> Nørre Farimagsgade 41, 1364 København K
<u>Phone:</u> +45 8993 8409
Höst Website
https://www.facebook.com/restauranthoest/
Höst Map
https://goo.gl/maps/GUxkxAEpWv52

12

Special Things to Do only in Copenhagen

Here's a list of unique experiences you can only have in this great city.

Check out the Frederiksborg Palace north of Copenhagen.

There's nothing quite like it. Surrounded by a lake and a beautiful garden, the construction of the Frederiksborg Palace began in the 1600s under King Christian IV. Stroll down the romantic Palace Garden.

Address: Møntportvejen 10, 3400 Hillerød
Frederiksborg Palace Website
http://www.dnm.dk/UK/Forside.htm
Frederiksborg Palace Map
https://goo.gl/maps/D42BJE7eheA2

Explore the Freetown Christiania.

Discover an alternative way of life by the inhabitants of this free town. Check out the homemade houses, organic eateries, art galleries and green neighborhood. Before entering Christiana, you will find a list of 'do's and don'ts' abide by these rules.

Copenhagen's green and car-free neighborhood

Among the things worth checking out are the Christiana Black-smith, the Christiana Cykler, the Grey Hall, the Gay House and Morgenstedet. You can also have lunch at Spiseloppen.

Enjoy the beauty of nature at the Botanical Garden.

Enjoy the peace and stillness at the 10-hectare garden. Check out the historical glass houses. There are 27 of them. Among the most visited is the one at the Palm House built in 1874. It stands 16 meters tall. The passageway to the top is paved by cast-iron spiral stairs.

Address: Øster Farimagsgade 2B, 1353 København K
Phone: +45 3532 2222
Freetown Christiania Map
https://goo.gl/maps/2AmuRWVXSnN2

Discover something new at the Experimentarium City.

It's going to be a fun and interesting tour especially for kids and the kids at heart. Experience science in action and in all its forms; satisfy your curiosity and enjoy the outdoor activities.

Experimentarium city is also a good place for a waterfront view of The Opera, The Royal Danish Playhouse and the Nyhavn. You can also enjoy some of the best street foods Copenhagen has to offer in this location.

Address: Trangravsvej 10-12, 1436 København K
Phone: +45 3927 3333
Experimentarium City Website
http://en.experimentarium.dk/
Experimentarium City Map

https://goo.gl/maps/hiFBvUHsp2A2

Observe at The Round Tower.

This is Europe's oldest functioning observatory built in the 17th century. Discover why the tower has made great astronomical achievements. See it for yourself. The Round Tower also houses a library hall where H.C. Andersen used to visit. There is also a glass floor where visitors can stand in and see the tower's core.

Address: Købmagergade 52A, 1150 København K
Phone: +45 3373 0373
Observe at The Round Tower Website
http://www.rundetaarn.dk/en/
Observe at The Round Tower Map
https://goo.gl/maps/NR8tQGjUmcs

Visit Carlsberg.

Your trip to Copenhagen won't be complete without a visit to this world famous brewery. Find out how Carlsberg makes their beer. Visitors can even sample Carlsberg products while enjoying a view of the copper vessels.

<u>Address:</u> Gamle Carlsberg vej 11, 1799 København V
<u>Phone:</u> +45 3327 1282
Carlsberg Website
http://www.visitcarlsberg.dk/
Carlsberg Map
https://goo.gl/maps/CMEzAU34ZwT2

Amalienborg Palace

If you have extra time in Copenhagen, then be sure to go and see the changing of the guards at the royal palace.London(UK) is not the only country in Europe with a Royal family and a changing of the guards.Amalienborg is the home of the Danish Royal family.The Royal Guards march from Rosenborg Castle(11:30 am) to Amalienborg Palace(12:00 pm).The changing of the guards ceremony starts at Amalienborg Palace at 12 pm every day.

Phone:+45 33 12 21 86
Address: Amalienborg Slotsplads 5, 1257 København K
Amalienborg Website
http://www.kongernessamling.dk/en/amalienborg/palacesquare/
Amalienborg Map
https://goo.gl/maps/AMUjrGuwhkF2

13

3-Day Itinerary

Day One – Copenhagen

6:30am Breakfast at the hotel

9:00am Begin your tour at the bronze statue of the spinner of fairy tales, Hans Christian Andersen at the Town Hall Square or Rådhuspladsen.

9:30am Walk along the 18th century houses at Lavendelstræde and see where Mozart and Constanze used to live

10:00am Walk along Slutterigade to see the city's law courts which used to be town hall built in 1805 and 1815

10:30am Walk past the 19th century houses at Nytorv

11:00am Check out Copenhagen's shopping district at Strøget

12:30 pm Lunch Break

1:30pm Continue the tour at Copenhagen's Oldest Church, Helligåndskirken, built in the 15th century

2:00pm Check out Christian IV's bronze replica of the 1688 sculpture at Kongens Nytorv

2:20pm Stop by for pictures at the Nikolaj Kirke from the 1530s.

2:40pm Visit the equestrian statue of Copenhagen's founder, Bishop Absalon at the Højbro Plads where you can also enjoy a stunning view of the Thorvaldsens Museum on Slotsholmen.

3:10pm Enjoy a panoramic view of the Christiansborg Palace from the Gammel Strand.

3:30pm Check out the old fashioned street of Snaregade.

4:00pm See the oldest structures in Copenhagen at the Magstræde, dating back to the 16th century.

4:30pm Head to the Tivoli Gardens. Check out the cafés and beer gardens there.

7:00pm Dinner at Geist

9:00pm Boat tour by the canal

Day Two

6:30am Breakfast at the hotel

9:00am Start at the "King's New Market" or Kongens Nytorv. Check out the Magasin, Copenhagen's biggest department store.

9:20am See the Thott's Mansion, originally built for a Danish naval hero, now houses the French Embassy.

9:40am Visit the Royal Theatre founded in 1748.

10:00am Take pictures at the baroque style building of Charlotten-borg Palace.

10:20am Check out Frederik V's statue and the residence of the queen and prince at the Amalienborg Palace.

10:40am Enjoy the view of the waterfront gardens at Amaliehavn.

11:10am Check out the marble church at Frederikskirke built in 1740.

11:30am Pay your respects to The Little Mermaid, the symbol of Copenhagen, near Den Lille Havfrue.

12:00nn Visit Amalienborg Palace for the changing of the guards.

1:30pm Check out where Hans Christian Andersen lived at no. 18, 20 and 67 at Nyhavn.

2:00pm Visit The Museum of National History.

3:30pm Head to Glyptoteket.

5:00pm Stop by for a quick bite at Café Glyptoteket.

6:30pm Visit The National Gallery of Denmark.

8:00pm Dinner at a Copenhagen restaurant of your choice.

10:30pm Check out one of the beer pubs or nightclubs.

Day Three

6:30am Breakfast at the hotel

9:00am Explore Christiana

11:00am Early Lunch

12:30pm Check out The Round Tower

1:30pm Visit the Botanical Garden

2:30pm Visit Carlsberg

5:00pm Go on a Shopping Spree

7:00pm Dinner at a restaurant of your choice

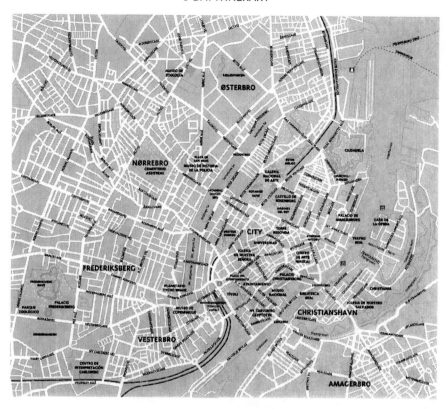

14

REYKJAVIK INTRODUCTION

I want to thank you for downloading this travel guide.In this travel guide, I have put together the best Reykjavik has to offer for anyone visiting but who have limited time in the city.This guide puts you a click away from the best of the best the city has to offer.So if you have a long weekend in Reykjavik, then this guide will make your stay a lot easier.

As the coastal capital of Iceland, Reykjavik serves as the country's cultural, financial, and government center. To the more or less 130,000 residents, it doesn't fall short of the magnificence that it is known to reward; it's no surprise that for a growing number of tourists from all corners of the globe, it's a well-visited destination.

With all sorts of business districts, restaurants that offer mouth-watering delights, shopping centers, and loads of unique hubs, not a lot of people have the courage to turn down an invitation.

I hope you have a great time in Iceland!

Good Luck!

15

History

History

As national records and various books about medieval settlements can attest, a Nordic named Ingolfur Arnarson is Reykjavik's first settler. In the early days, particularly in 870 AD, he built and established and a home in the sea; he would then follow wherever the water, which flowed around the area, took him. Since he was considered high authority, he was the one who baptized the place with a name; he called it Reykjavik that can be translated as "steam cove" or "stone cove".

Nationalism, the War, & the Fight for Independence

In Reykjavik, life remained rather fundamental throughout the centuries until the later years of the 1800s; then, the voices that yearned for any form of national pride started to come out. A general assembly named "Althingi" was formed, which pushed the official establishment of Reykjavik as the country's capital.

By then, the city, somehow, found an identity of its own; it armed itself with a constitution and continued to gain executive power. Consequently, different industries (e.g. sulfur mining, fisheries, agriculture, wool, etc.) were gradually built, and each one began to emerge. However, troops from Germany, Denmark, Britain, and the US came to invade the place. It wasn't only until 1944 that the declaration of full independence was granted.

After the War

From the late 1900s onward, Reykjavik saw further developments as a city. Since it extended an effort to participate in global competitions, it started to earn international recognition. For one, representatives were sent to join in a major chess tournament in 1972.

And, like others who were seen in the international scene, Reykjavik was associated with a string of financial crises, economic crashes, and government feuds. Nonetheless, it held onto its establishment by remaining strong as a city.

The Reykjavik of Today

Today, Reykjavik may already have developments in place, but it continues to achieve better grounds; as a city, it aims to be a more pleasant place and its government wants to do good for its people. It hopes to reward residents with an increasing number of outstanding establishments. Alongside, it makes sure that locals can enjoy their while with rich and colorful experiences.

Consequently, visitors from across the globe can benefit from the cause, too.

So far, Reykjavik is in the pursuit of contributing a touch of its locality to worldwide audiences; it is known for being the home of artists, comedians, writers, and notable personalities. Among the list are Halldor Laxnesss, Bjork, Yrsa Sigurdardottir, Arnaldur Indridason, Bubbi Mortens, and Sigur Ros.

16

Entering Reykjavik

An airport in Reykjavik is usually the first place a tourist finds himself in, once he arrives in the city. There, he begins to figure out where to go in the following moments.

Keflavík International Airport (Icelandic: Keflavíkurflugvöllur)

Like him, you may find yourself in a Reykjavik airport once you decided to tour the city. Especially if you're travelling solo, you may be a bit anxious or overwhelmed at the adventure that's ahead of you. But, don't worry, granted that you arranged air travel weeks or even months before your Icelandic escapade. Since you're already in the fascinating city, the next thing for you to do is to give yourself a warm welcome.

Keflavik International Airport Website
http://www.kefairport.is/english/
Phone:+354 425 6000

Keflavik International Airport Map
https://goo.gl/maps/WG6c5NxaD4t

The Airport Express bus service between the airport and both Reykjavik and Akureyri. I recommend you book this bus service online before you arrive.

Keflavik International Airport Transport
https://airportexpress.is/
Phone:+354 540 1313
Email:iceland@grayline.is

List of airports that are located close to Reykjavik:

- Domestic Reykjavik Airport
- Akureyri Airport
- Husavik Airport
- Saudarkroukur Airport
- Vestmannaeyjar Airport
- Vopnafjordur Airport

List of major airlines that offer flights to Reykjavik:

- Air Berlin
- Air Greenland
- Air Iceland
- Delta
- Easy Jet
- Scandinavian Airlines
- WOW Air

Transportation in Reykjavik

The different means of transportation in Reykjavik will make you realize that hopping from one local spot to another is rather easy. Since the place is small, waiting for a ride that can take you to a particular destination can happen in a snap of a finger.

Additionally, another option is walking around Reykjavik; you may want to bike around, too. Remember that the city is tiny, which means that primary local attractions are located within close proximity to each other. Sure, it can be exhausting, but if you're open to the idea, don't set it aside. First, you can experience the place's splendor better; for another, you can reduce transportation costs this way.

Bike Tours and Rental Website
http://www.icelandbike.com/
Bike Tours and Rental Map
https://goo.gl/maps/z3PwXjzZjc12
Phone:+354 694 8956

Available transportation options:

A great investment for your Reykjavik trip is The Reykjavik City Card or The Reykjavik Welcome Card; the list of options includes costs of 1,900 ISK for 24-hour bus services, 2, 400 ISK for 36-hour bus services, and 2, 900 ISK for 72-hour bus services. Although it is rather expensive, previous visitors, regular tourists, and locals agree that is worth the purchase. Apart from offering convenience when it comes to navigating the city, it privileges the card holders to loads of freebies and discounts.

List of inclusive freebies:
- Access to The Reykjavik Museum in Asmundarsafn
- Access to The Reykjavik Art Museum in Hafnarhus
- Access to The Reykjavik Art Museum in Kjarvalsstadir

- Access to The National Gallery of Iceland
- Access to The Reykjavik Zoo & Family Park
- Access to certain hot springs and public thermal pools

List of inclusive discounts:
- Fish Company (10% discount)
- Rossopomodoro (10% discount)
- Reykjavik Restaurant (10% discount)
- Saga Museum Tour (10% discount)
- Whale-watching in Elding (10% discount)
- The Phallological Museum (20% discount)
- Volcano House (20% discount)
- The 360 Cinematic Experience at Expo Pavilion (20% discount)
- Seltjarnarnes Thermal Pool (50% discount)
- Kopavogur, Kopavogslaug Thermal Pools & Salalaug (50% discount)

- Loft Hostel
- The Icelandic Travel Market

- Borgartun Guest House
- Laugardalur Campsite
- Hilton Reykjavik
- Fosshotel Lind
- Kvosin Supermarket
- Tourist Information Center

Straeto or Reykjavik's Public Transportation System

Straeto or Reykjavik's Public Transportation System is a local bus company that can grant you the opportunity to explore different places with the city. As the regulations go, first, you need to purchase a ticket inside the bus (for about 300 ISK), followed by a skiptimidi or a transport ticket.

One you secured tickets, you can enjoy the privilege of seeing the most fascinating sites in the city. And aboard a bus, you can roam around the area as you wish – whether you want to visit random spots or you have a specific destination in mind.

Car Rental Stations

For about 2, 500 ISK per day (or above), you can bring additional privacy to your in Reykjavik by availing of the services car rental stations. Especially if you want to get around in the city with a monster truck (or mostly a selection of 4 x 4 jeeps), a chance to have your own ride seems a comforting option.

On a related note, be aware that in Reykjavik's highlands, there's only a single station that sells diesel and petrol. You may need to keep this information in mind to avoid running out of fuel in the middle of the (sometimes) isolated roads. So long as your tank is full or has sufficient gas for your trips, getting around in a car is a fun alternative.

List of companies that offer affordable car hire:
- Adventure Rentals
- Atak Car Rental
- Geysir
- Hertz
- Europcar
- SADCARS
- Thorcars
- Happy Campers
- Sixt

17

Safety

Reykjavik's tap water.

The Icelandic tap water is among the first concerns of some tourists as soon as they step foot in the city. While others refuse to risk the chance of filling their systems with unfiltered, "faucet water", many go right ahead and "dive in" by drinking the city's ordinary water.

Especially those who have done their research about Reykjavik's water system? They're not oblivious to the truth that the tap water in the city is safe to drink. Although it may smell a little like rotten eggs, it's very unlikely for you to end up in a health center after you hydrate yourself with the local tap water. And, for what it's worth, the unpleasant odor that strings along is merely the smell of sulfur or geothermal hot water.

In fact, if you're that tourist who goes inside a convenient store and comes back outside after having purchased a bottle or two of commercial water, don't be surprised at the sight of locals' glares; chances are, you're a subject of their laughs.

Nonetheless, Reykjavik's tap water is just a side concern.

Safety (on the Road)

112 are the emergency digits, and ICE-SAR, or Icelandic Search & Rescue is the emergency team in Reykjavik (and in all areas across Iceland); if you need reinforcements, give the hotline a call. In a jiffy, roadside assistance will be provided. Especially if you get around in a private car, and you ran out of gas, you were distracted by the magnificent views of your surroundings, or other unexpected circumstances, keeping in mind the channels for contacting emergency services can be useful.

Notes regarding safety:

The right-hand lane is the primary driving lane

The Icelandic dogs, the Icelandic sheep, the Icelandic horse, reindeers, arctic foxes, and other domestic animals are often seen on city roads; slowing down is recommended.

Since there are plenty of blind summits, embankments (i.e. road-side barriers against the snow), and one-lane bridges, a slow driving speed, and extreme caution are recommend.

While cars are in operation; headlamps are required to be switched on

Speed limits vary according to conditions and places; the limits are: (1) in gravel roads, 80 km/h, (2) in small areas, 90 km/h, and, (3) in urban places, 50 km/h.

Crossing rivers in the city inside a car isn't unusual for locals; it should be accomplished with 4 x 4s only, such as pick-up trucks and jeeps.

Safety (Medical Emergencies)

Because of the city government's high regard for a clean and green environment, Reykjavik is a top contender in a list of European places with the healthiest people; more than 80% of taxes is allotted to healthcare and medical services. Visiting the cool area in Iceland is unlikely to post any health-related risks. But, just in case of physical accidents or any emergency that requires immediate medical attention, the Landspitali University Hospital in the central region is the place to go to.

<u>Climate</u>

Climate and weather conditions in Reykjavik can be problematic; it's rather unpredictable. It's usually cold in the city, but when it's sunny, the places can be disheveled by a storm quickly. Also, during night times, the surroundings can seem cool (average), but the temperature can eventually drop to freezing point without warning.

However, so long as you: (1) prepared for the conditions, (2) wear layers of clothes, and (3) packed the appropriate accessories such as a thick jacket or trench coat, gloves, boots, leg warmers, and ear puffs, you'll be fine.

18

Reykjavik for Tourists

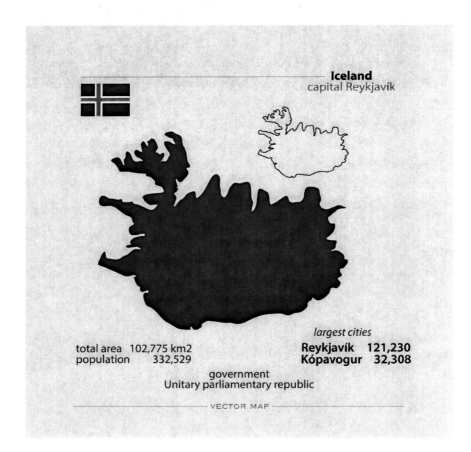

Iceland
capital Reykjavík

largest cities
Reykjavík 121,230
Kópavogur 32,308

total area 102,775 km2
population 332,529

government
Unitary parliamentary republic

VECTOR MAP

Reykjavik for Tourists

Víðsýni (pronounced as vee – yo – si – ni) is an Icelandic word that means "to keep an open mind". It can be a great term for Reykjavik tourists to ponder on since it serves as a reminder for them to immerse into the sometimes odd yet enriching culture of the city; granted that they're open to exploring the different corners around them, splendor awaits.

While shaking your head to say "no", or nodding to say "yes" could work for you when you're in Reykjavik, it's best to have basic knowledge of some Icelandic words and phrases. For one thing, head gestures can be misleading; for another, a simple lesson on the native tongue is a no-brainer. In fact, you could even keep a notebook for jotting down the useful terminologies and bring it with you on your trip; the collection will come in handy. And, for the record, "na" is Icelandic for "no, and "já" is for the word "yes".

Table of Icelandic terminologies for tourists:

Icelandic word or phrase
English translation

Hallo
Hello

Takk
Thank you

Bless
Goodbye

Enskou talarou?

Can you understand English?

Islenkku eg talla ekki
I don't understand Icelandic

Flugvollur
Airport

Umferoarmiostoo
Bus station

Koma
Arrival

Brottfor
Departure

Bilaleiga
Car rental service

Bokun
Reservation

Hvar er
Where is

Hvert fara?
Where will you go?

Einn mioa till
A ticket to

Hvao mikio?

How much?

Takið þið krítarkortum?
Are credit cards acceptable?

Ég mundi kaupa (insert name of product).
I am interested in buying (insert name of product).

Since a memorable trip in Reykjavik isn't likely free, be ready with some Icelandic Krona or ISK. From your budget, make a plan and strategize regarding the distribution of your cash. Fortunately, products and services in the region are priced reasonably. But, nonetheless, especially if you plan to experience the best of the city, you need to start the conversion from your local currency to the city's money.

According to overseas.com, a website that features sample

itineraries for tours to several places, a 3-day trip to Reykjavik can amount between 45, 000 ISK and 50, 000 ISK. It depends on your preference, but the estimated cost includes roundtrip airfare (to and from an American destination), (4 sets of meal per day), accommodation at a quality yet affordable hotel, hiking, horseback-riding, sight-seeing at more than 20 key local attractions, and souvenir-shopping – all for 3 days.

1 ISK = 0.0068 EUR (Euro)
1 ISK = 0.92 JPY (Japanese Yen)
1 ISK = 0.0048 GBP (British Pound)
1 ISK = 0.0075 USD (American Dollar)

500 kronur
1000 kronur
2, 000 kronur
5, 000 kronur
10, 000 kronur

1 kronur
5 kronur
10 kronur
50 kronur
100 kronur

Tip: Know about the Best Time to Visit

Did you know that there is a day when Reykjavik residents only experience 4 hours of sunlight? With the city being only 2 degrees on the southern area of the Arctic Circle, you wouldn't be caught off guard by the information.

In a related manner, a visit to Reykjavik is best done during the summer season. Then, sunlight is most likely to last 24 hours, and according to the locals, there are instances during this period that the sun doesn't fully set. Especially if you don't fancy the idea of night trips, the months of May, June, July, and August are the ideal months for an adventure.

Whether you're a returning visitor, or a first-timer, a trip to Reykjavik can be an unforgettable experience. Compared to your home, the environment may be a notch different. For instance, upon your arrival, you may find it rather odd why there are heaps of people in the city, and why the rest of the surrounding regions seem uninhabited.

So, instead of getting too intimidated of certain practices, as well as to maximize your trip in the city, keep in mind a number of facts.

Majority of the locals call each other by their first name, and majority of people call each other similarly. The reason? They do not have a surname; the suffix -son (i.e. somebody's son) or -dottir (i.e. somebody's daughter) is added (e.g. eionsdottir, ragnarson, gnarrsdottir, etc.).

Carrying credit cards or debit cards, in favor of tangible Icelandic Krona, is the way to go in Reykjavik; that's how locals go around. It's not due to the possibility of getting cash stolen from you, contrary to the tranquil place's reputation, it's just how the system functions; most restaurants, convenient stores, entertainment centers, and hotels are known to accept major cards.

Icelandic cars are often monster trucks (i.e. huge jeeps with huge tires), which is one of the top things that bother first-time visitors. Although it's a common joke that it's because of their owners' inferiority complexes, a reason behind the gigantic size of the locals' ride is the ability to pass rough terrains.

Babies (i.e. children in strollers) are usually left outside of cafes and dining centers. Since crimes are hardly ever committed in the city, and in the entire country, locals tend to be considerate, trust-worthy, and respectful toward their fellows.

Nudity isn't rare; locals usually don't mind seeing people walking on the streets without clothes on. For them, it's no big deal to enter public pools and hot springs naked and some of them even make showering together a practice. In fact, Reykjavik is associated with the #freethenipple hashtag, which was a call for a topless revolution in early 2015.

"Reykjavik, best i heimi!" means "Reykjavik, the best in the whole world!" it is a popular catch-phrase in Reykjavik. Apart from the fact that locals remind their fellows that they are in the best destination in the world, it is a chant to let a tourist know that the most thrilling sites are just there for him to explore.

Facts that can support the claim that Reykjavik (and Iceland as a nation) is home of the best? According to guidetoiceland.is (and a number of articles online) that compared the city to other places in the world, it is the home of: (1) the most number of musicians and artists, per capita, (2) the happiest people, per capita, and (3) the best handball team, per capita. When it comes to its residents, did you know that the world's strongest men, per capita, are from the region? Also, four Miss World candidates are from the area.

To top it all off, Reykjavik has the most beautiful centers within walking distance of each other.

"Reykjavik, best i heimi!" means "Reykjavik, the best in the whole world!" it is a popular catch-phrase in Reykjavik. Apart from the fact that locals remind their fellows that they are in the best destination in the world, it is a chant to let a tourist know that the most thrilling sites are just there for him to explore.

Facts that can support the claim that Reykjavik (and Iceland as a nation) is home of the best? According to guidetoiceland.is (and a number of articles online) that compared the city to other places in the world, it is the home of: (1) the most number of musicians and artists, per capita, (2) the happiest people, per capita, and (3) the best handball team, per capita. When it comes to its residents, did you know that the world's strongest men, per capita, are from the region? Also, four Miss World candidates are from the area.

To top it all off, Reykjavik has the most beautiful centers within walking distance of each other.

19

Hotels

The Reykjavik Eco Campsite

The Reykjavik Eco Campsite, situated 3 kilometers from the city's central district, is an option when spending a night or two in Reykjavik. Although it appears like most camping grounds, your experience will be more like first-level camping, as the site is categorized as a 5-star hotel.

If you think that it's you're risking the chance of poor accommo-dation by choosing the Reykjavik camping ground, you're mistaken. As a 5-star hotel, it offers a range of facilities and services; the list includes a swimming pool, bicycle station, and diner. Also, available is free Wi-Fi and parking.

Especially if you're traveling Reykjavik on a budget, gathering your tents, sleeping bags, comforters, and other camping gears, as well as your outdoors spirit, is worth considering.

Address: Sundlaugavegur 32, 105 Reykjavík
Phone:+354 568 6944
Reykjavik Eco Campsite Website
http://www.reykjavikcampsite.is/
Reykjavik Eco Campsite Map
https://goo.gl/maps/xnUYcnXcxir

Hotels in Reykjavik: Should You Stay in One?

If you want to skip the idea of camping in Reykjavik, staying in a hotel is a great alternative.If you're on a tight budget, you can still get sufficient rest (and pampering) since there is a line-up of affordable hotels in the city. All you need is to be mindful of the inclusive services, and, of course, their star ratings.

The list of basic services and facilities (for 1-star hotels):

Rooms with shower and bath
Rooms with colored TV & remote control
Room cleaning (daily)
Soap

Desk and chair
Reception services
Public telephone
Deposit possibilities

2-Star Hotels in Reykjavik

According to the European Hotel Union, a 2-star hotel in Reykjavik means that it offers standard accommodation. Particularly, it means that (in addition to the services and facilities offered by 1-star hotels) it provides: (1) breakfast buffet services, (2) linen shelves, and bath essentials, (3) sanitary products, (4) and desk and lamp for bedside reading. Apart from that, it accepts credit cards when it comes to payment. For a budget-friendly and worthwhile trip in the cool city, a booking in a standard hotel seems a good option.

The list of top 2-star hotels in Reykjavik:

Airport Inn

Address: Airport Inn
31 Soleyjagata
101, Reykjavik
Rates: 11, 500 ISK (on average, per 24 hours)
Phone:+354 456 4444
Airport Inn Website
http://www.airportinn.is/
Airport Inn Map
https://goo.gl/maps/8BRhTMe3BKr

Reykjavik Hostel Village

Address: Reykjavik Hostel Village

1 Flokagata
Reykjavik
Rates: 10, 500 ISK (on average, per 24 hours)
Phone:+354 552 1155
Reykjavik Hostel Village Website
http://www.hostelvillage.is/
Reykjavik Hostel Village Map
https://goo.gl/maps/xpkemicNtPL2

Bus Hotel Reykjavik

Address: Bus Hotel Reykjavik
105 Skogarhlio
Reykjavik
Rates: 21, 900 ISK (on average, per 24 hours)
Phone:+354 535 0350
Bus Hotel Reykjavik Website
http://www.bushostelreykjavik.com/
Bus Hotel Reykjavik Map
https://goo.gl/maps/hPf7Pz4aU9n

Stay Apartments Boholt

Address: Stay Apartments Boholt
6 Boholt
105 Reykjavik
Rates: 23, 900 ISK (on average, per 24 hours)
Phone:+354 517 4050
Stay Apartments Boholt Website
https://stay.is/
Stay Apartments Boholt Map
https://goo.gl/maps/RNMTq3pi2w82

Hostel B47

Address: Hostel B47
101 Baronsstigur
101, Reykjavik
Rates: 18, 500 ISK (on average, per 24 hours)
Phone:+354 458 9000
Hostel B47 Website
http://www.hostelb47.is/
Hostel B47 Map
https://goo.gl/maps/XfBihD55SxR2

Loft Hostel

Address: Loft Hostel
7a Bankastraeti
101, Reykjavik
Rates: 13, 900 ISK (on average, per 24 hours)
Phone:+354 553 8140
Loft Hostel Website
http://www.lofthostel.is/
Loft Hostel Map
https://goo.gl/maps/fjvhTaCUvvH2

Hotel Gardur

Address: Hotel Gardur
29 Hringbraut
101, Reykjavik
Rates: 20, 600 ISK (on average, per 24 hours)
Phone:+354 511 1530
Hotel Gardur Website
http://hotelgardur.is/

Hotel Gardur Map
https://goo.gl/maps/xRaq7NyowKx

Hotel Viking

Address: Hotel Viking
Strandgotu, Ibrattohusio
202, Reykjavik
Rates: 19, 900 ISK (on average, per 24 hours)
Phone:+354 565 1213
Hotel Viking Website
http://fjorukrain.is/
Hotel Viking Map
https://goo.gl/maps/tTdafP5BamN2

North Star Apartments

Address: North Star Apartments
Hamrabog
202, Reykjavik
Rates: 19, 000 ISK (on average, per 24 hours)
Phone:+354 566 7979
North Star Apartments Website
http://northstar.is/
North Star Apartments Map
https://goo.gl/maps/zWQzJiWY7Q82

Guesthouse Vikingur

Address: Guesthouse Vikingur
20 Overholt
Reykjavik
Rates: 17, 600 ISK (on average, per 24 hours)

Guesthouse Vikingur Website
http://guesthouse-vikingur.hotelreykjavik.net/en/
Guesthouse Vikingur Map
https://goo.gl/maps/DFgVEyvFVCP2

3-Star Hotels in Reykjavik

3-star hotels in Reykjavik, according to the European Hotel Union, are considered comfort hotels. It means that (in addition to the services and facilities offered by 1-star and 2-star hotels), it includes: (1) luggage service and 3-pc suite, (2) bilingual staff at reception, (3) room telephone, (4) beverages inside room, (5) heating facility, (6) internet access, (7) sewing kit, (8) dressing mirror, (9) additional pillows and comforters on demand, and (10) complaint management system.

The list of top 3-star hotels in Reykjavik:

Arctic Vik Comfort Hotel

Address: Arctic Vik Comfort Hotel
N Haaleiti
Reykjavik
Rates: 20, 900 ISK (on average, per 24 hours)
Phone:+354 588 5588
Arctic Vik Comfort Hotel Website
http://www.arcticcomforthotel.is/
Arctic Vik Comfort Hotel Map
https://goo.gl/maps/hwcNqSbofgB2

Apartment K

Address: Apartment K

Bingholtstraeti 2
Reykjavik
Rates: 45, 000 ISK (on average, per 24 hours)
Phone:+354 578 9850
Apartment K Website
http://www.apartmentk.is/
Apartment K Map
https://goo.gl/maps/RsXZSTDWq682

Leifur Eiriksson Hotel

Address: Leifur Eiriksson Hotel
45 Skolavoroustigur
101, Reykjavik
Rates: 29, 400 ISK (on average, per 24 hours)
Phone:+354 562 0800
Leifur Eiriksson Hotel Website
http://www.hotelleifur.is/
Leifur Eiriksson Hotel Map
https://goo.gl/maps/CLX6VKqGem12

Fosshotel Lind

Address: Fsshotel Lind
Raudarararstigur, 18
105, Reykjavik
Rates: 13, 000 ISK (on average, per 24 hours)
Phone:+354 562 3350
Fosshotel Lind Website
http://www.fosshotel.is/hotels/fosshotel-in-reykjavik/fosshotel-lind/
Fosshotel Lind Hotel
https://goo.gl/maps/EpeDEFxbMqw

Fron Reykjavik Hotel

Address: Fron Reykjavik Hotel
22A, Laugavegur
101, Reykjavik
Rates: 15, 000 ISK (on average, per 24 hours)
Phone:+354 511 4666
Fron Reykjavik Hotel Website
http://www.hotelfron.is/
Fron Reykjavik Hotel Map
https://goo.gl/maps/cuH1Cm3rN5r

Reykjavik Lights

Address: Reykjavik Lights
Suourlandsbraut 16
Reykjavik
Rates: 25, 000 ISK (on average, per 24 hours)
Phone:+354 513 9000
Reykjavik Lights Website
http://www.keahotels.is/en/hotels/reykjavik-lights
Reykjavik Lights Map
https://goo.gl/maps/4VGntZsiZpB2

OK Hotel

Address: OK Hotel
74 Laugavegur
101, Reykjavik
Rates: 35, 000 ISK (on average, per 24 hours)
Phone:+354 578 9850
OK Hotel Website
http://www.hotelreykjavik.net/

OK Hotel Map
https://goo.gl/maps/sL5CuAi8YFB2

Cabin Hotel

Address: Cabin Hotel
32, Borgartun
105, Reykjavik
Rates: 19, 300 ISK (on average, per 24 hours)
Phone:+354 511 6030
Cabin Hotel Website
http://hotelcabin.is/
Cabin Hotel Map
https://goo.gl/maps/bsvbUDbNEp22

20

Restaurants

Restaurants

Restaurants in Reykjavik aren't only known for the mouth-watering dishes they offer; they're also a stand-out when it comes to meals that are prepared with a notoriously challenging approach (e.g. wind-drying, transhumance farming, etc.). There may be a number of restos around you; you can try each one, but if you can, head to the best ones first.

The list of 5 of the best restaurants in Reykjavik:

Baejaryns Beztu Pylsur
Address: Baejaryns Betzu Pylsur
1 Tryggvagotu
101, Reykjavik
Phone:+354 511 1566

Baejaryns Beztu Pylsur, first serving locals in 1937, is a famous hotdog stand in downtown Reykjavik. It makes hotdogs with the combination of beef, pork, and lamb; the list extends to raw and cooked onions, sweet mustard, ketchup, and remoulade.

A tourist who goes to Reykjavik (or in nearby regions of Iceland) makes it a priority to try the local hotdog – the local hotdog that is dubbed Europe's best hotdog. In fact, prominent personalities are known to adore the hotdogs; two of them are Metallica's James Hetfield and America's president, Bill Clinton.

Baejaryns Beztu Pylsur Website
http://bbp.is/en/
Baejaryns Beztu Pylsur Map
https://goo.gl/maps/SLehWLmiY4x

Grillmarkadurinn
Address: Grillmarkdurinn
2a Laekjagarta
101, Reykjavik
Phone:+354 571 7777

Since it went into business in 1920 (even after its original location got burned down), Grillmarkadurinn has been delighting locals and tourists with regional dishes. Like its name suggests, it serves grilled favorites made of meat and fish; for the more adventurous bunch, remember that puffin, whale steak, and reindeer burgers are all part of its menu. Plus, it offers a selection of wines and cocktails that may not be found anywhere else.

With Gudlaugur Frimannson and Hrefna Rosa Saetren, and other respected chefs in Reykjavik, Grillmarkadurinn continues to be a legendary restaurant in the city.

Grillmarkadurinn Website
http://www.grillmarkadurinn.is/
Grillmarkadurinn Map
https://goo.gl/maps/gNHA8z2kxPq

Hradlestin
Address: Hradlestin
8 Laekjagarta
101, Reykjavik
Phone:+354 578 3838

Cod curry and smoked samosas, and other classic Indian favorites are served with a flavor of Icelandic cooking in Reykjavik's Hradlestin; spicy cocktails accompany the dishes. Locals consider it among the top diners in the area because of its distinct style. What's more is that each meal is presented in a metal tiffin box. For tourists who want to have a taste of Indian cuisine and Bollywood-themed environment, it's the ideal restaurant.

Hradlestin Website
http://en.hradlestin.is/

Hradlestin Map
https://goo.gl/maps/Jr3k8LKr2312

MAR Restaurant
Address: MAR Restaurant
9 Gelrsgata
101, Reykjavik
Phone:+354 519 5050

MAR Restaurant is the go-to of Reykjavik locals who are craving for South European and South American delights. Among its menu offerings are pan-fried lobsters, Madelra truffle glaze, and mushroom risotto; it also provides an extensive list of wines.

MAR Restaurant Website
http://www.marrestaurant.com/
MAR Restaurant Map
https://goo.gl/maps/v2kJCb9KvAn

Salt Eldhus
Address: Salt Eldhus
1 Laugavegur
101, Reykjavik
Phone:+354 551 0171

Salt Eldhus, owned by Tilefni Audur Orn, is a known restaurant in Reykjavik; it's linked to its traditional cooking such as farmhouse favorites, home-made bread, and home-made soup. A reason why locals prefer to visit regularly if that it offers simple, light snacks that reminds them of what Icelandic flavors are made of. Also, did you know that is culinary school? That being said, not only can you have a serving of delicious meals, you can also learn while you're around.

Salt Eldhus Website
http://www.salteldhus.is/en
Salt Eldhus Map
https://goo.gl/maps/inpappuQJe62

21

Museums and Art Galleries

Bakari Galeri

With a location in a famous bakery, Bakari Galeri is an art gallery that exhibits the latest artworks; it is where the works of renowned artist-designers such as Erro and Gotti Bernhoft are featured. There, you can spend hours checking out kaleidoscopic pieces, cartoon-style works, spray-painted art, colorful graffiti, and even art covers for rock bands.

Address: Bakari Galeri , 14 Bergstadastraeti ,Reykjavik
Phone:+354 551 3524
Bakari Galeri Website
http://sandholt.is/
Bakari Galeri Map
https://goo.gl/maps/c9sRSbvVSF32

Icelandic National Gallery

The emphasis of the art collection is on 19th and 20th-century Icelandic art.They also have a good international art collection.

Address: 7, 101 Reykjavík, Iceland
Phone:+354 515 9600
Icelandic National Gallery Website
http://www.listasafn.is/
Icelandic National Gallery Map
https://goo.gl/maps/3F611i1JnWL2

Kling and Bang

Kling and Bang is an art gallery led by a batch of Reykjavik's finest artists. Since its establishment in 2003, it stayed true to its mission of supporting individuals who have a knack for creative thinking. As it is today, it's a big player in the city's art scene; it is home to the works of Margret Helga Sesseljudottir, Emma Helloasdottir, and other local artists, as well as German artists.

Address: Kling and Bang ,42 Hverfisgata ,Reykjavik
Phone:+354 696 2209

Kling and Bang Website
http://this.is/klingogbang/index.php?lang=en&
Kling and Bang Map
https://goo.gl/maps/mJv8nkAHibL2

The Museum of Living Art

The Museum of Living Art, a non-profit art gallery, welcomed its first visitors in 1978; then, its establishment was intended to compete with Iceland's National Gallery. It showcases artworks made with a variety of mediums that stir people's normal thinking. There, you can find poetry readings, painters' live performances, and script screenings.

Address: The Museum of Living Art ,28 Skulagata , 101, Reykjavik
Phone:+354 551 4350
The Museum of Living Art Website
http://www.nylo.is/
The Museum of Living Art Map
https://goo.gl/maps/t7GgBPCx5UU2

The Nordic House

The Nordic House is deemed one of Reykjavik's icons; since it was designed by the legendary Finnish modernist and architect, Alvar Aalto, tourists are known to stop by regularly to simply look at the structure. On the outside, the place and its setting are already breathtaking.

On the inside, The Nordic House features eclectic line-ups of works from international artists such as Jonathan Josefsson and Guany Hafsteinsdottir. If that's not awesome enough, take note that the art gallery is also a place that serves an assortment of delicious foods and drinks.

Address: The Nordic House, 5 Sturlugata , 101, Reykjavik
Phone:+354 551 7030
The Nordic House Website
http://nordichouse.is/
The Nordic House Map
https://goo.gl/maps/yZMKEnQ3inA2

22

Bars & Clubs

With the number of Reykjavik locals who goes out late, it's a perk that the city has tons of bars and clubs. A great thing about these places is that they don't impose too many rules (e.g. dress codes, cover charges, etc.); so long as you're at least 20 years old (the legal drinking age in the region), a fun and wild night is yours to expect. For a tourist who prefers his or her trip to be worthwhile, as well as to be part of Reykjavik's way of life, you may want to spend an hour or so at the top night hubs.

Kaffibarinn

Address: Kaffibarinn
1 Bergstaoastraeti
Reykjavik
Phone:+354 551 1588

Kaffibarinn is associated with excellent DJs and friendly staff. There, you and Reykjavik locals can unwind by ordering famous Icelandic drinks such as Reyka, Opal, Icelandic Vodka, and Topas. Also, you may find the trivia that it serves as a coffee shop in the morning useful.

Kaffibarinn Website

https://www.facebook.com/kaffibarinn
Kaffibarinn Map
https://goo.gl/maps/FRzWUDtTTwy

Kormaks Olstofa og Skjaldar

Address: Kormaks Olstofa og Skjaldar
Olstofan
4 Vegamostatig
Reykjavik
Phone:+354 552 4687

Kormaks Olstofa og Skjaldar, popular for its own home-made beer named Brio, is a bar for people who prefer the simple things in life. There, the crowd is usually made up of writers, artists, and musos. And, there, you won't find a dance floor and sound system.

Kormaks Olstofa og Skjaldar Website
https://www.facebook.com/OlstofaKormaksogSkjaldar
Kormaks Olstofa og Skjaldar Map
https://goo.gl/maps/hBHCsADhH3T2

Micro Bar

Address: Micro Bar
6 Austurstrati
Reykjavik
Phone:+354 776 6687

The bar for beer nerds is Reykjavik's Micro Bar; it's a microbrewery that supports local brewers and small beer businesses. After you find a stool, you can hang around and enjoy a selection of beers including one named Tactical Nuclear Penguin.

Micro Bar Website
http://microbarreykjavik.wixsite.com/micro
Micro Bar Map
https://goo.gl/maps/tBe5st2wsnM2

Snaps

Address: Snaps
1 Porsgata
Reykjavik
Phone:+354 511 6677

Snaps is a place for serving cool refreshments and an affordable meal. While satisfying you with food and drinks, you can check out the distinct surroundings; hanging plants can be found in the venue. And, to toss in a trivial thing, a piano that is free for the public to use is just around the corner.

Snaps Website
http://www.snaps.is/
Snaps Map
https://goo.gl/maps/hGvqRKvSFLy

23

Shopping

Shopping Districts

When it comes to shopping in Reykjavik, Laugavegur is the street where you want to go. From books, CDs, DVD, figurines, and other collector items to clothes, jewelries, and all sorts of accessories, you can find almost anything. Therefore, if you want to take home the best souvenirs when you head outside of the city, make sure to stop by the top shopping districts first.

Laugavegur Street Map
https://goo.gl/maps/decVU7UMR4p

The list of 4 of the best shops in Reykjavik:

Dogma

Address: Dogma
30 Laugavegur
Reykjavik
Phone:+354 562 6600

If going through a selection of items such as weird and funny t-shirts, unique slogans, comical sweaters, bacon lip balms, and squirt cameras is what you will enjoy, Reykjavik's Dogma is the store for you. Since the staff are known to be quite approachable, you can engage in a fun chit-chat with an employee regarding the things you're about to purchase.

Dogma Website
http://www.dogma.is/en/home
Dogma Map
https://goo.gl/maps/caPNSzq4vZn

Kolaportid

Address: Kolaportio
19 Tryggvagata
Reykjavik
Phone:+354 562 5030

Kolaportid is Reykjavik's locals go-to when they plan to get their hands on cheap but quality stuff. There, you can take home vintage records, clothes, shoes, books, and house ornaments; a purified shark is also for sale. If you can't decide on what to buy, but you feel the need to buy something, perhaps, a stroll in the place considered the city's flea market will give you an idea.

Kolaportid Website
http://www.kolaportid.is/Index.aspx?lang=en
Kolaportid Map
https://goo.gl/maps/18Nov5yHsrN2

Spilastofa and Verslun

Address: Spilastofa and Verslun
2 Ingolfsstraeti
Reykjavik

If you're a proud nerd, Spliastofa and Verslun is the shop you need to go to. There, you can purchase classic superhero figurines, toys, retro t-shirts, mugs, posters, and more. Again, if collecting certain items from comics, video games, books, films, and TV is your passion, take the time to stop by the place; not everywhere can you find the items sold inside.

Spilastofa and Verslun Website

https://www.facebook.com/freddireykjavik
Spilastofa and Verslun Map
https://goo.gl/maps/dxK8w9c6KZM2

Tiger

Address: Tiger
13 Laugavegur
Reykjavik
Phone:+354 660 8201

Tiger is a favorite Danish retail store of Reykjavik locals. A reason why it's a top-visited place is that it offers random items that can be used by family members. Also, almost everything you can buy inside costs cheap.

Tiger Website
http://www.tiger-stores.com/
Tiger Map
https://goo.gl/maps/gu7FbuWsAU82

24

Only in Reykjavik

Isruntur

Isruntur is an Icelandic term that means ice cream drive; it describes the activity of going on a road trip while eating ice cream. Since most people are fond of ice cream, this may not seem a stand-out.

However, it is; it somehow defines the incredible love of locals in Reykjavik for ice cream. It's loved so much that it's not a rare event to see them having ice cream for breakfast, ice cream for lunch, ice cream for snack time, and ice cream for dinner. While there may be people who'd rather pass up the opportunity to eat ice cream when it's cold, the ones in the city are unlikely to decline an offer to have a cone, pint, or gallon of ice cream.

Certainly, there are more weird things that Reykjavik locals are known for. If you think about it, since they're people who lived in isolation for a thousand years, this isn't surprising. And, apart from the rare stuff, there are normal activities to do in the city, too.

Odd, Just Odd!

Although they are quite embarrassing and are the type of things that make you question your sanity, taking part in some of the Reykjavik's locals wicked ways is likely to make your Icelandic escapade memorable. There are plenty of once-in-a-blue-moon opportunities while you're in the city, so you may want to consider going nuts for a couple of days. In fact, as many tourists said, refusing to go with the flow can be regrettable.

List of odd things to do in Reykjavik:

Pee in the Sea

"You're new to Reykjavik, I can tell," is a statement that you're bound to hear if you haven't (or will not) pee in the sea. Moreover, urinating suggests that you're one with the people in the city. You may find it unsanitary, but the practice can make you feel like a Reykjavik local.

Have a sheep's head for dinner

In Reykjavik, The Coach Terminal is the place where you can feast on a sheep's head, or Kjammi og Kok; it is a dish you may be interested in trying since it's not every day that you get a chance to have a ginormous skull for a meal. If you prefer to have an extra satisfying dinner, an order of beef stew and a can of super cold Coke is the way to go.

Take home Reykjavik's landi

Landi is an alcoholic drink that you can buy secretly from hardcore teens in Reykjavik; it's home-made brew that rewards a psychedelic experience. But just so it's clear, you should know that if you're caught with a bottle or two, you'll possibly get in trouble with the authorities of Fangelsismalastofnun rikisins (or the Icelandic Prison system); having the drink is illegal!

Visit the Penis Museum

If you're in Reykjavik, you might as well stop by the Phallological Museum of Iceland, or Iceland's penis museum. If you didn't know it's the only one in the world, then, now you do. There, you'll find more than 200 exclusive penises of mice, goats, and whales. There's even a human penis on display.

Address:Laugavegur 116, 105 Reykjavík
Phone:+354 561 6663
Penis Museum Map
https://goo.gl/maps/HVDpp7Cr1Em

Average Activities

Admiring street art is an average activity of Reykjavik locals; residents of the city don't even have to head to specific streets for the art works since they're almost everywhere. If you're the type who wants to roam around and let your feet take you to spontaneous destinations that are nothing short of marvelous, it's an ideal mundane activity for you, too.

List of other average things to do in Reykjavik:

Bathe in the Blue Lagoon

The Blue Lagoon is the place to go to when you're in Reykjavik; it's the # 1 tourist destination in Iceland. There, not only will you find a breath-taking lagoon and skincare spa, but you'll also find Lava Restaurant, Lagoon Bar, and Blue Café. With limited accommodation, make sure that you book advance tickets at Blue Lagoon Ticket Center.

Technically, the Blue Lagoon isn't located in Reykjavik; it's in Grindavik. However, since it's about less than an hour drive from the city, why not make an exception?

Address:Álfheimar 74, 104 Reykjavík
Phone:+354 414 4004

Blue Lagoon Website
http://www.bluelagoon.com/
Blue Lagoon Map
https://goo.gl/maps/mx91D99Hepr

Check out the Solfar

The Solfar, or the Sun Voyager is a stainless steel sculpture that you can find in the middle of Reykjavik waters. Rumors emerged that say it's a Viking ship or a boat where pirates reside; to know what the structure really is, why not check it out yourself?

Moreover, the Solfar is a sculpture that symbolizes a dream of progress, hope, and freedom; it was created by Jon Arnason as a reminder to strive for development. Usually, the sight of it rewards inspiration for a fresh and better outlook in life.

Address:Sculpture & Shore Walk, Reykjavík
Solfar Map
https://goo.gl/maps/dAELRJ3KzuK2

Drive along the Golden Circle

When you drive along the 300-kilometer route called the Golden Circle, among the attractions you'll see are Gulfoss Waterfall, Strokkur, Geysir Hot Springs, Thringvellir Lift, and Hverageoi Greenhouse Village. With all the wonders you can visit, a grand road trip (from Reykjavik, Iceland's central region, and back to Reykjavik) is yours.

Phone:+354 511 2600
Golden Circle Tour Website
https://www.re.is/day-tours/the-golden-circle
Golden Circle Tour Map
https://goo.gl/maps/LnQa9oLfsyJ2

Hang out at Reykjavik's Family Park & Zoo

At Reykjavik's Family Park & Zoo, dolphins, grey seals, arctic foxes, reindeers, Icelandic dog, Icelandic sheep, and Icelandic horses are among the animals who have found a home. Other than that, the place features a humongous trampoline, small racetrack, cute bulldozers, boats, bounce houses, slides, and more.

Address:Hafrafell v/ Engjaveg,
Laugarnesvegur, Reykjavík
Phone:+354 575 7800
Family Park & Zoo Website
http://www.husdyragardur.is/
index.php/english123
Family Park & Zoo Map
https://goo.gl/maps/LNq4wYxWCAr

Hike at Landmannalaugar

Landmannalaugar is the portion of Fjallabak Reserve in Reykjavik's highlands. It's the place where you are granted a heavenly view of the city below; it's the place to go to if you want to see the panoramic landscapes, wildlife, mountain air, and geothermal hot springs, or the natural beauty of the cool place you're in. And, if you're a hiker, it's the ideal trail.

Phone:618-7822
Landmannalaugar Website
http://www.landmannalaugar.info/
Landmannalaugar Map
https://goo.gl/maps/XsbWwo92ExG2

Visit Hallgrimskirkja

Hallgrimskirkja, a Lutheran Chapel, is considered one of the tallest buildings in Reykjavik; it also serves as an observation tower. It's worth seeing since its expressionist architectural style is unlike any other.

Even if you are not Lutheran (or associated with any religious sector), the chance to visit Hallgrimskirkja is not one you want to miss. Otherwise, you'll pass up opportunities to lay eyes on a gigantic pipe organ, Leif Eriksson Statue, and the majestic views of the colorful houses and establishments in Reykjavik.

Address:Hallgrímstorg 101, Reykjavík
Phone:+354 510 1000
Hallgrimskirkja Website
http://www.hallgrimskirkja.is/english/
Hallgrimskirkja Map
https://goo.gl/maps/fgnsny8zWcB2

Visit the Imagine Tower

The Imagine Tower, or Fridarsulan, is a column that serves as a memorial for Yoko Ono's late husband, John Lennon; it is located in Viðey Island, which is almost part of Reykjavik. Underneath, there are roughly a million wishes (written on paper) by the widow over the years.

If you're going to visit Reykjavik, and you plan to stop by the Imagine Tower, the days from October 9 to December 8 are worth considering; they're the days when the tower is lit. Once lit, it showcases a light exhibition that consists of more than 10 searchlights; the exhibition usually reaches cloud base and can be viewed all across Iceland.

Imagine Tower Website
http://imaginepeacetower.com/
Imagine Tower Map
https://goo.gl/maps/S8kzw1LdpJJ2

25

3-Day Itinerary

Reykjavik is one of the epitomes of the idea that says "life comes in small packages"; the city may not be as vast as other places, but a visit is worthy of being jotted down in most people's bucket lists. It is full of scenic settings; just about everywhere you turn to, you'd be in awe. So, be sure that your journey in the city is unforgettable, and what better way to do so than to prepare an itinerary?

Once you're checked in at a quality Reykjavik hotel, packed a bunch of clothes, prepared a share of Icelandic krona, and everything else you need (maybe including a camera), you can let your adventure commence.

Day 1 in Reykjavik:

A Warm Welcome to Reykjavik
- Drive along the Golden Circle
- Lunch at your choice of restaurant
- Hang out at Reykjavik's Family Park & Zoo
- Check out the Solfar
- Dinner at your choice of restaurant

Day 2 in Reykjavik: Blending with a "Cool" Way of Life
- Walk around; check out Reykjavik homes and street art
- Lunch at your choice of restaurant; hang out at a nearby sea (and

pee in the sea)
- Bathe in the Blue Lagoon
- Dinner at the Coach Terminal (and have a sheep's head for dinner)
- Visit the Phallological Museum of Iceland and other galleries of your choice
- Hang out at your choice of bar/nightclub

Day 3 in Reykjavik: The Final Hurrah

- Hike at Landmannalaugar
- Visit Hallgrimskirkja
- Shop for souvenirs
- Dinner at your choice of restaurant
- Visit the Imagine Tower

26

STOCKHOLM INTRODUCTION

Sweden is a beautiful country in Europe that is rich in history, art, and culture, and its capital Stockholm is in the heart of its continuing legacy. Over the years, this majestic capital has grown in popularity among tourists. In fact, in 2010 alone, Stockholm welcomed more than ten million overnight stays, which made it the most visited city in all of Scandinavia. People are drawn to the natural beauty of Stockholm, what with it being named Europe's first ever Green Capital by the European Union (EU) Commission. Tourists also come to this city to learn more about the medieval era, of which Stockholm has many stories of. The city's countless museums and art galleries also add to the appeal, and its good food, good beer, and vibrant nightlife put it on top of many people's Must-Visit Cities in Europe list.

If you appreciate nature, love art, and crave delicious food, then Stockholm, Sweden is the right travel destination for you. In just three days, Stockholm will take you on a journey through ages, beginning with its roots in the medieval times and ending with its current position in the contemporary world through its art. Your palette will also enjoy this vacation because Stockholm is the home of comfort food and crazy concoctions. Moreover, if those things are not enough, take pleasure in and unwind with the beautiful view of the city's harbor and well-kept parks.

Through this travel guide, you will find short lists of the best of the best in Stockholm. From affordable accommodations to the most popular restaurants to the museums and galleries you just can't miss, this book has got you covered. Find activities to do and places to visit; be excited by the nightlife and satiate yourself with a cup of fika (coffee). There is even a three-day itinerary included at the end of this book to give you an idea of how much you can do while visiting this beautiful and historical European city.

Note, also that all prices listed on this book are rounded to the nearest dollar value. I hope that this will make budgeting for your travel a lot easier.

And so, without further ado, here is your travel guide for your short-stay travel here in Stockholm, Sweden.

27

History of Sweden

For 2000 years (8000 B.C. to 6000 B.C.), the land that is now Sweden was the main hunting, gathering and fishing grounds for ancient people who used simple stone tools. Numerous artifacts that were used in the Nordic region during the Bronze Age had been found all over the country, with some even dating as far back as 1800 B.C. This marks the beginning of Sweden's history.

Fast forward to more than a thousand years later, in 500 B.C., when the land dwellers had settled in the area, and agriculture became the prominent backbone of the society. Stone tools were phased out, and iron tools replaced them quickly.

The Viking Age of Sweden didn't happen until much later, around 800 A.D. to 1050 A.D., when expeditions started moving towards the east. Traders traveled to the Baltic coast, with some even reaching as far out as the rivers of what is now the territory of Russia. Thievery and plunder were prominent during this era, when the region was yet to be introduced to religion.

The spread of religion and Christianity did not happen until the 9th century when a man named Ansgar came to the country with a mission to convert Vikings to believers. For two centuries, citizens fought back and restrained from religion, and it was not until the 11th century that Christianity successfully and widely influenced the region.

Around this time, the previously segregated provinces in the region were also combined into one territory. However, only in 1280 did King Magnus Ladulås authorized the establishment of noble families, marking the early roots of the monarchy in Sweden.

Economy and trade boomed during the first half of 14th century when German traders (called the Hanseatic League) brought goods and services to Sweden. However, the impressive and continuous rise of economy suddenly took a hit when the Black Death plagued the country in 1350. Both economy and population took a steep decline during this devastating time.

It was also during the fourteenth century that the Kalmar Union was established in Scandinavia. Denmark, Norway, and Sweden were congregated under Danish Queen Margareta's rule in 1389. From the late 14th century to the early 16th century, however, the Kalmar Union brewed internal conflicts between the three nations, and by 1520, the problem had gone out of hand when 80 members of the Swedish noble family were sentenced to die at the inauguration of Kristian II, then King of the Union. This event was later referred in history as the Stockholm Bloodbath.

A year later, Gustav Vasa, a member of the Swedish noble family, led the rebellion against the King of the Union. Kristian II was killed during the battle, and Gustav Vasa was then proclaimed King of Sweden, two years after the rebellion began.

Gustav Vasa reigned Sweden from 1523 to 1560. This is referred to as the Vasa Period in Sweden's history. During his reign as King, the crown took the church, and the monarchy was officially established as the way of governance in the country.

The 1600s was a great century for Sweden. They won several wars, including their victory against Denmark in the Thirty Years' War, and they also accumulated quite a few territories in Europe, including some provinces in the northernmost regions of Germany. They even had a small colony in present-day Delaware in the United States. The Baltic republics were also under Sweden's command. And, after proclamations of peace (of Westphalia in 1648 and of Roskilde in 1658) between Sweden and Denmark, this nation was considered one of the (if not the) greatest monarchy in the entire continent.

However, its prominently agrarian economy failed its ability to stay in power. After the Great Northern War of the early 1700s, Sweden lost its territories on the other side of the Baltic Sea. It lost again during the Napoleonic Wars, and had to surrender Finland to Russia, which was its last colony during this era.

In 1810, a French marshal Jean Baptiste Bernadotte was named heir to the crown. Four years later, he was successful in absorbing Norway into Sweden's regime. However, almost a century later, the two countries had a lot of internal disagreements that, ultimately, led them to part ways.

The 18th and 19th centuries marked a further decline in the country's economy and population. After its great loss in the Napoleonic Wars, the parliament decided to abolish the governmental rule of the Royal Family, but its trade and commerce were not at all helped by their decision to overhaul the government system. Citizens moved out of the country, and those who remained were still earning their wages through farming.

It was not until after World War II that Sweden experienced a rapid growth. In fact, its growing industrialism post-war made it one of Europe's fastest growing countries during this time.

Today, Sweden remains a beautiful country that has rich culture, art, and history.

28

Travel Season and Weather

Stockholm, Sweden is best visited during the summer. Although hotel rates and airfares may get a lot more expensive during this season, the city is a lot livelier and more vibrant than the rest of the year. Daylight can last for 24 hours during the summer months, giving you more time to explore the history, culture, and arts of Stockholm. The temperature in the warm season range between 68 and 71 degrees Fahrenheit during the day, and can drop to 10 to 20 degrees Fahrenheit at night.

However, if you are more interested in watching a few winter sports during your stay in the city, then it is best to visit around December to February. Less people travel to Stockholm during these months, which means the city is not as crowded as it is in the summer. You will find public transportation a lot easier during the winter, and hotels are not as booked as they are when the tourism in the city is at its peak.

If you want to learn more about the city's travel season and weather, below is a more detailed description of what you can expect for each month of the year in Stockholm.

January

January is the middle of winter in Stockholm, Sweden. You can enjoy many winter activities, as detailed in Chapter 12 of this travel guide. Also, January is when hotel rates and airfares get a lot cheaper. The holidays are over, so there are fewer tourists and smaller crowds. In other words, if you visit the city in January, you can experience Stockholm when it's relatively peaceful and quiet.

February

February is the month of winter sports. People come to watch and participate in winter sports including skiing, sledding, and snowboarding. You can also rent snowmobiles and ride through the snow. And though February is the coldest month of the year in Stockholm, the almost freezing temperature is worth it because of the frequent view of the Northern Lights.

Aside from the winter sports, February is the month of the Vikingarännet, or the Viking Run. The Vikingarännet is an ice-skating race event. Its course runs through Stockholm and Uppsala, which is another city in Sweden 44 miles north of its capital.

<u>March</u>

Days start to get longer and warmer in Stockholm during March. The winter slowly transitions into the beautiful green landscape that the city has. It is also during this month that the annual Vildmarksmässan, or Wildlife Fair, is held. The Wildlife Fair is an outdoor show with lots of different sporting events and activities.

The temperature in March is still pretty cold, ranging between 20 to 30 degrees Fahrenheit. Airfares and hotel rates will start to go up at the beginning of spring, but they are still a lot cheaper than they are during the summer.

April

April is your last chance to see the Northern Lights. It usually appears until late April, before it disappears for the rest of the year once again. April is also the month of Walpurgisnacht, or the Walpurgis Night, which is the eve of Saint Walpurga's feast day. During the Walpurgis Night, people have bonfires and dances on the streets, singing traditional spring folk songs loudly to ward off evil spirits.

May

Spring blooms in full during May. Parks and attractions open up to welcome both locals and tourists. There are also a lot of activities in Stockholm during this month. One of them is the Gärdesloppet, or the Gärde Race, which is a racing event for 1920s cars.

June

June is the beginning of summer in Stockholm. It marks the

upward trajectory of the city's tourism as well. People from all over the world visit Stockholm because of its open-air events and attractions. They also stay for the midnight sun, a natural occurrence where the sun remains visible in the sky even at midnight. During this time, there is pretty much daylight for 24 hours, given that the weather conditions remain fair. This makes it a good time to explore the city and soak in its beauty. It is also when Scandinavians celebrate the Midsummer Festival, or the festival of the summer solstice.

Moreover, Smaka På Stockholm, or "A Taste of Stockholm", happens in June. It is an annual food festival in the city that attracts more than 350 thousand visitors from all over Sweden, Europe and the world.

July
July is usually the warmest month of the city. It also means that Stockholm is most crowded during this time of the year. Aside from the breathtaking view, the historical landmarks, and the countless museums and art galleries in the city, people come to Stockholm also for the largest Pride Parade in Scandinavia. Since it first began in 1998, participants and supporters have grown dramatically in Stockholm. In fact, in 2014, 60 thousand people came to participate and a whopping 600 thousand more followed the parade on the streets.

August

Because it is the last month of summer in Stockholm, hotel rates and airfare are still pretty expensive during August. But don't get disheartened; there are still a lot of things you can do in Stockholm to make your visit worthwhile. One of the most awaited events during August is Propaganda, a music festival arranged to highlight both established and upcoming musicians from Sweden and the rest of Europe. It is open to audiences aged 13 years and above. However, in order to get to the bar area, you must be at least 18 years old.

September

September is when Stockholm starts to get quieter. Its mild temperature makes it a good time to visit the city if you want to avoid crowds. Hotel rates and airfares also start to dwindle, averaging at $30 a night for a 3-star hotel.

Many events also happen during September. One of them is the Stockholm Beer and Whiskey Festival, which is usually held late September until early October. During this festival, you can attend several liquor and beer tastings and master classes.

Tjejmilen, or Ladies' Mile, is another event that is held in September. It is the largest sporting event for women in all of Sweden. Annually, it attracts more than 30 thousand participants from all over the country and the continent, and it happens usually at the beginning of the month.

Lastly, the Stockholm Half-Marathon is held usually in the first or second week of September. It has a 21.1-kilometer course (about 13 miles) that runs through some of the best tourist spots in Stockholm.

October

Prices continue to drop in October, but the weather is still good for travel. The temperature averages at about 50 degrees Fahrenheit during this month. Fewer people also visit during October, and so, if you have a small budget and a fear of big crowds, October is a lovely time to visit the city.

November

Ski resorts in Stockholm begin to open at the start of winter, which is November. Winter activities and sports become an attraction for tourists who love spending time in the snow. It is the best time to come to Stockholm if you want to experience the city in winter but are not willing to pay the expensive holiday rates during December.

December

If you wish to know what a Scandinavian Christmas is like, then you should obviously come to Stockholm in December. Prices may hike up a lot, but it will be worth the cost just to see the Northern Lights in the sky. You can also enjoy the holiday season by doing some winter activities such as skiing and sledding. And for a better picture of what you can do during the winter in Stockholm, make sure to read Chapter 12 of this book.

29

Transportation Options

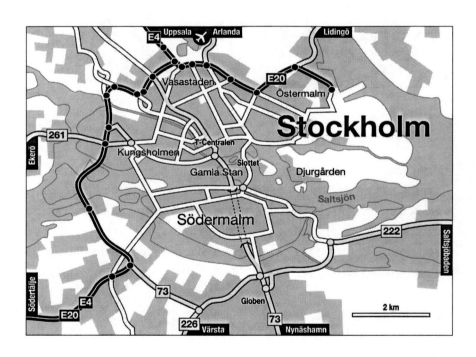

Stockholm Map
https://goo.gl/maps/j16nVHzNsRy

Airports

Stockholm has three major airports: the Stockholm Arlanda Airport, the Bromma Stockholm Airport, and the Stockholm Skavsta Airport (also known as the Nyköping Airport). You can also get to Stockholm from the Stockholm Västerås Airport (also known as the Hässlö Flygplats), which is located in the city of Västerås, about 68.5 miles west of Stockholm.

Stockholm Arlanda Airport Website
http://www.swedavia.com/arlanda/#gref
Stockholm Arlanda Airport Map
https://goo.gl/maps/e5w3Acvr3QQ2
Phone:+46 10 109 10 00

Bromma Stockholm Airport Website
http://www.swedavia.com/bromma/#gref
Bromma Stockholm Airport Map
https://goo.gl/maps/5J3d9hqVefn
Phone:+46 10 109 40 00

Stockholm Skavsta Airport Website
http://www.skavsta.se/en/
Stockholm Skavsta Airport Map
https://goo.gl/maps/4N8NRXztZN82
Phone:+46 155 28 04 00

Stockholm Västerås Airport Website
http://www.vst.nu/engelska-sidor/vasteras-airport.html
Stockholm Västerås Airport Map
https://goo.gl/maps/ds1vmM1e23k
Phone:+46 21 80 56 00

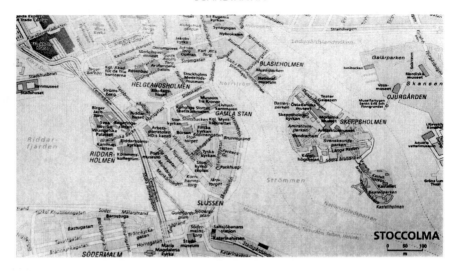

How to Get to Stockholm's City Center from These Airports

You have three options on how to get to the city center
of Stockholm from the

- Arlanda Express Train: Located just below the arrival terminals,
  the Arlanda Express Train will take you to the city center in the
  fastest time. Trains leave every 15 minutes, and travel time will
  take only about 20 minutes.

Arlanda Express Train Website
https://www.arlandaexpress.com/contact.aspx
Phone:+46 771 720 200

- **Flygbussarna Airport Coaches**

Flygbussarna Airport Coaches Website

http://www.flygbussarna.se/en

Phone:0771-51 52 52

- **Train Station**

Arlanda Central Station Map

https://goo.gl/maps/dbJMqT1CM382

Transportation from the Bromma Stockholm Airport

- Flygbussarna Airport Coaches: Just like at the Stockholm Arlanda Airport, Flygbussarna Airport Coaches operate on these three other airports in Stockholm. Travel time to the city center from the Bromma Stockholm Airport is 20 minutes, while that from the Stockholm Skavsta Airport or the Stockholm Västerås Airport is 80 minutes. Departure times of the Flygbussarna Airport Coaches vary, depending on the departure and arrival schedules in these three airports.

Flygbussarna Airport Coaches Website

http://www.flygbussarna.se/en/customer-services

Phone: 0771-51 52 52

00 46 771 51 52 52

- If you do not opt to travel via bus or train, you can always take a cab from the Stockholm Arlanda Airport and the Bromma Stockholm Airport. Depending on the time of the day, travel from the Stockholm Arlanda Airport to the city center via taxi takes about 40 minutes, while travel from the Bromma Stockholm Airport to the city center via taxi takes about 15 minutes.

Note, also, that cab fares in Sweden are not regulated. Therefore, different cab companies may have different fare rates. To make sure your cab driver does not scam you, Stockholm's official website suggests that you only take a ride on cabs operating under Taxi 020, Taxi Kurir, and Taxi Stockholm. These taxi firms are well-established in Stockholm because of their good services and reasonable prices. They also accept credit card payments.

Public Transportation

The Stockholm Public Transport (SL) controls the city's public transportation system. It has two types of tickets, both of which are used in all of SL's public transportation services.

Public Transportation Website
http://sl.se/en/
Metro 2

https://www.mtr.com.hk/en/corporate/consultancy/
stockholmmetro.html

(1)Zone tickets are used for short trips. They only last for an hour after they are stamped, but you can use them if you plan to transfer into another form of public transport. You can purchase zone tickets as cash tickets (available at train and bus stations, and also from conductors), pre-paid tickets (single units and 16-unit slips available at resellers, 16-unit slips also available at train and bus stations), text message tickets (via mobile purchase, and is valid for 15 more minutes, as margin for the time of purchase), and vending machine tickets (via ticket machines in select bus and train stations, paid with card or coins).

(2)Travel cards are suggested for tourists who plan to go around the city a lot. They can last for 24 hours to up to a year, depending on which type you purchase. They are valid across SL zones, and can be bought in SL centers around Stockholm.

If you're planning to use zone tickets instead of buying a travel card during your stay in Stockholm, then you should know about SL's zone system. Basically, SL divided the city in three zones, with Zone A covering the city center and most of the inner suburbs, Zone B covering the area between Zones A and C, and Zone C covering most of the outer suburbs.

If you want to travel through these zones, you will need different zone tickets. You will also need additional tickets if you want to travel to zones outside the border of Stockholm (for example in Bålsta or Gnesta). The latter holds the case even if you purchased a travel card.

For your short-stay travel, it is suggested that you purchase a 3-day travel card. It is priced at about $28 for people between 20 and 65 years old. If you are younger or older than those age restrictions, you will only have to pay about $17.

For zone tickets, the following is a breakdown of prices. Note: Discounted prices, again, are for people younger than 20 years old and older than 65 years old.

(1)Cash Tickets

Regular price per unit: $3.00
Discounted price per unit $2.00

(2)Pre-paid Tickets

Regular price per unit: $2.25
Discounted price per unit: $1.50
Regular price per 16 units: $23.75
Discounted price per 16 units: $13.00

(3)Text Message Tickets and Vending Machine Tickets

Regular price for 1 zone: $4.25
Discounted price for 1 zone: $2.50
Regular price for 2 zones: $6.50
Discounted price for 2 zones: $3.50
Regular price for 3 zones: $8.50
Discounted price for 3 zones. $4.75

Experience Stockholm on a Bicycle

One of the best ways to experience Stockholm is on a bike.You can rent a bicycle and ride around the bike paths all over the city.
Bicycle Website
http://www.rentabike.se/
Bicycle Map
https://goo.gl/maps/pLr3Vy3yKyq
Phone: +46 8 660 79 59

30

Best Affordable Hotels

Traveling to Sweden does not have to be expensive. For your short-stay travel in Stockholm, here are the top 5 affordable hotels around the area.

Connect Hotel Stockholm

Location: Alströmergatan 41, 112 47 Stockholm, Sweden
Tel:+46 8 441 02 20
Starting Price: $29.25
Rating: 3 Stars

From the Connect Hotel Stockholm in Götalandsvägen, it only takes two train stops via the Pendeltág train for you to get to the center of the city. From there, you can explore Stockholm's famous landmarks, such as the Riddarholmskyrkan, which is the oldest building in the Stockholm. The hotel has 95 modern-styled rooms, and you can choose whether you want to have bunk beds with shared bathrooms or double beds with a private bath. You can also find a lounge, a restaurant, and a bar/café inside the hotel.

Connect Hotel Stockholm Website
http://connecthotels.se/en/
Connect Hotel Stockholm Map
https://goo.gl/maps/HiBsRHacVCv

Rex Petit Hotel

Location: Luntmakargatan 73, 113 51 Stockholm, Sweden
Tel:+46 8 23 66 99
Starting Price: $35
Rating: 2 Stars

If you like to discover Stockholm's vibrant media and music scene, then the Rex Petit Hotel is the best accommodation for you. Located in the city center in the Vasastaden district, it is only a short walk away from famous Stockholm musical landmarks such as the Opera House. The streets around the hotel are also famous for its nightlife. You can find a lot of restaurants, bars, cafés, and clubs in the area.

The Rex Petit Hotel is relatively small compared to the other hotels on this list. With only 22 rooms, you can choose between bunk beds that come with private bathrooms or double beds that have communal bathrooms.

Rex Petit Hotel Website
http://rexpetit.se/en/Rex_petit
Rex Petit Hotel Map
https://goo.gl/maps/CdzbkoVWBYM2

Scandic Ariadne

Location: Södra Kajen 37, 115 74 Stockholm, Sweden
Tel:+46 8 517 386 00
Starting Price: $43.50
Rating: 3 Stars

The Scandic Ariadne has a simple yet cozy aesthetic that makes travelers feel at home. It has 283 private bedrooms with en suite bathrooms, as well as a few superior, more spacious bedrooms that feature a mini bar.

The hotel also has a restaurant (the Mistral) and a bar (the Sky Bar) within its premises. Both of these venues have terrific views of Stockholm; from the Mistral, you can sit on the terrace that overlooks the harbor, and from the Sky Bar, you have a view of the city skyline.

The Stockholm Central Station is just 6 minutes away from the Gärdet metro station, which is a 15-minute walk away from the hotel. But if you will rather take the bus to get to other places in the city, the Ropsten metro station is also close by.

Scandic Ariadne Website

https://www.scandichotels.se/hotell/sverige/
stockholm/scandic-ariadne
Scandic Ariadne Map
https://goo.gl/maps/CfoGdAWckMS2

Scandic Bromma

Location: Brommaplan, 168 76 Stockholm, Sweden
Tel:+46 8 517 341 00
Starting Price: $50
Rating: 2 Stars

You can choose from the Scandic Bromna's 144 cozy private bedrooms. All of their units come with an en suite bathroom and a shower.

Stockholm landmarks that are close to the Scandic Bromna include the breathtaking Drottningholm Palace, which has been declared a UNESCO Heritage Site. This tourist spot and the Stockholm Airport are just about 2 miles away from the hotel. You can also reach the city center in about twenty minutes by taking the bus.

Scandic Bromma Website
https://www.scandichotels.se/hotell/sverige/stockholm/scandic-bromma
Scandic Bromma Map
https://goo.gl/maps/rqHhWZgH5fR2

Scandic Park

Location: Karlavägen 43, 102 46 Stockholm, Sweden
Tel:+46 8 517 348 00
Starting Price: $52.25

Rating: 3 Stars

The Scandic Park is conveniently located in the center of Stockholm. It has 201 private bedrooms that come with en suite baths. From the hotel, you can have a view of the beautiful Humlegården Park, which is a major park in the district. In the Humlegården Park, you will find the Royal Library and a statue of Linnaeus (Carl von Linné), who is a famous Swedish scientist. The Stockholm Stadium is also a short distance away, while the Stadion metro stop is a 3-minute walking distance from the hotel.

Scandic Park Website
https://www.scandichotels.se/hotell/sverige/stockholm/scandic-park
Scandic Park Map
https://goo.gl/maps/8Ay6rekK7qF2

31

Best Restaurants

An important part of any culture is its food, and what better way to get to know Stockholm than to experience its delicious cuisine. Here are the top 5 restaurants in the city.

Gro

Location: Sankt Eriksgatan 67, 113 32 Stockholm, Sweden
Opening Hours: 5:30 P.M. to 11:00 P.M. Tuesday – Saturday
Phone:+46 8 643 42 22
Price Range: $58.75 for a four-course meal

If you are especially fond of eating vegetables (or in Swedish, grönsaker, which means "green things"), then Gro is the restaurant for you. Here, head chefs Henrik Norén and Magnus Villnow present locally grown vegetables and ingredients in an elevated manner. One of their specialty dishes uses cauliflower in several unique ways—puréed, roasted, pickled, and raw—and you can enjoy such creative dishes like this one at Gro every day during lunch. (Unfortunately, the restaurant is currently serving dinner every Thursday only.)

Gro Website
http://grorestaurang.se/
Gro Map
https://goo.gl/maps/DTFGTzukvwM2

Lilla Ego

Location: Västmannagatan 69, 113 26 Stockholm, Sweden
Opening Hours: 5:00 P.M. to 11:00 P.M. Tuesday – Saturday
Phone:+46 8 27 44 55
Price Range: $16.50 to $37.75

Lilla Ego may the priciest restaurant on this list, but it is absolutely worth it. Head chef Tom Sjöstedt and his business partner Daniel Räms were both awarded Chef of the Year and have now come together to create their own culinary masterpieces. In fact, the restaurant has risen in popularity since it opened on November of 2013. In order to secure a table at this famous yet unpretentious restaurant, you will have to book three months in advance.

Lilla Ego Website
http://www.lillaego.com/
Lilla Ego Map
https://goo.gl/maps/tAa9raEH4xB2

Nook

Location: Åsögatan 176, 116 32 Stockholm, Sweden
Opening Hours: 5:00 P.M. to 11:00 P.M. Tuesday – Saturday
Bar is open until 1:00 A.M. except on Tuesdays
Phone:+46 8 702 12 22
Price Range: $13 to $31.25

If you suddenly crave for a little Swedish and Asian fusion while in Stockholm, then you should definitely check out Nook. Head chef Claes Grännsjö was actually born in Korea, and so his menu items are inspired heavily by this country's cuisine. In Nook's menu, you will find traditional Swedish dishes like Torskrygg (cod) with ägg (egg), gröna ärtor (green peas), parmesan, and sardeller (sardines), along with unique Korean food items such as blood sausage.

Nook Website
http://nookrestaurang.se/
Nook Map
https://goo.gl/maps/XTQpjrkEUqx

Nytorget 6

Location: Nytorget 6, 116 40 Stockholm, Sweden
Opening Hours: 7:30 A.M. to 12:00 A.M. Monday – Tuesday
7:30 A.M. to 1:00 A.M. Wednesday – Friday

10:00 A.M. to 1:00 A.M. Saturday
10:00 A.M. to 12:00 A.M. Sunday
Phone:+46 8 640 96 55
Price Range: $18.25 to $27.75 (for main courses on their evening menu)

Its comfort foos and cozy atmosphere make Nytorget 6 such a delight to its customers. Because its main courses are priced very affordably, people are always coming back to enjoy what the restaurant has to offer. One of its most popular dishes is the råraka, a grated potato pancake cooked to a crisp and served with bleak roe, red onions, and sour cream. You can try Nytorget 6's råraka dish, or you can order their premium cut steak, served with chips, and drizzled with a little bit of béarnaise sauce.

Nytorget 6 Website
http://www.nytorget6.com/
Nytorget 6 Map
https://goo.gl/maps/iBzFT9EDony

Speceriet

Location: Artillerigatan 14, 114 51 Stockholm, Sweden
Opening Hours: 5:00 P.M. to 11:00 P.M. Monday and Saturday
11:30 A.M. to 2:00 P.M. and 5:00 P.M. to 11 P.M. Tuesday – Friday
Phone:+46 8 662 30 60
Price Range: Currently not listed on their website

Speceriet is located in the wealthy district of Östermalm in Stockholm, yet it's delicious food items have very affordable prices. It is no wonder why this quaint, little restaurant is popular to both locals and tourists, especially because its two head chefs, Jacob Holmström and Anton Bjuhr, are experienced in their fine-dining, Michelin-starred restaurant called Gastrologik. If you happen to come by the Östermalm district in Stockholm, make sure to try out Speceriet's fried pickled salmon, served on a crispbread with potatoes and caper mayonnaise.

Speceriet Website
http://speceriet.se/?lang=en
Speceriet Map
https://goo.gl/maps/dA3c9DFdJi62

32

Most Famous Landmarks

Learning about Stockholm's history and culture is as easy as visiting its most famous landmarks. Here are the 5 most famous landmarks in Sweden's capital. (Note: Admission fees are rounded up to the nearest dollar value.)

The City Hall

Location: Hantverkargatan 1, 111 52 Stockholm, Sweden
Opening Hours: 8:00 A.M. to 4:30 P.M. Weekdays
Admission Fees: $8.25 to $11.75

Stockholm's City Hall has always been a tourist attraction. At the peak of its 348-foot tower is a spire that holds the national coat of arms of Sweden, the golden Three Crowns. Designed by architect Ragnar Östberg, the building is considered a beacon of Sweden's national romanticism in architecture.

Today, the City Hall is home to the great Nobel banquet, a celebration that honors outstanding individuals from their respective fields. Offices and session halls can also be found behind the classic façade, where Stockholm's officials and politicians conduct their businesses.

The City Hall Map
https://goo.gl/maps/JUifkQY6Su42

Drottningholm Palace

Location: 178 02 Drottningholm, Stockholm, Sweden
Opening Hours: 10:00 A.M. to 4:30 P.M. Daily
Admission Fees: $14

Part of UNESCO's World Heritage List, the Drottningholm Palace
is the current home of Sweden's Royal Majesties, the King and the
Queen, and the rest of the Royal family. It was built in the 1600s and
designed by architect Nicodemus Tessin the Elder, who was chosen
by then Queen Hedvig Eleonora to lead the project. The south wing
of the palace is reserved for the Majesties' residences, but the rest of
the structure and the grounds are open to tourists and visitors. Inside
the Drottningholm Palace, you will find the Museum De Vries, which
is an outstanding collection of bronze sculptures created by Dutch
artist Adriaen de Vrie in the 1700s, and the Royal Chapel, which has
been the venue of numerous Royal events since 1746.

Drottningholm Palace Website

http://goo.gl/pzioCk

Drottningholm Palace Map

https://goo.gl/maps/vNhVbJPwVNs

Gamla Stan

Location: Gamla Stan, Stockholm, Sweden

Opening Hours: None

Admission Fees: None

Stockholm was first founded in 1252, in the beautiful town of Gamla Stan. Today, the Old Town, as both locals and tourists know Gamla Stan, serves as a reminder of Sweden's rich history. It is the biggest and most well-preserved medieval town in the entire continent, and it attracts international visitors with its historical architecture, as well as its abundant museums, bars, cafés, restaurants, and shopping centers.

If you visit Gamla Stan, you will have the chance to walk through beautiful cobblestone roads that wind through golden buildings and structures. Take a detour at Sweden's oldest square, Stortorget, and its oldest street, Köpmangatan. Around this area, you will also find the Stockholm Cathedral (Sweden's national church), the Royal Palace, and the Nobel Museum.

Gamla Stan Map
https://goo.gl/maps/9Ak25gj1DCq

Kungliga Operan
Location: Gustav Adolfs torg 2, 103 22 Stockholm, Sweden
Opening Hours: Varies between shows
Admission Fees: Varies between shows
Phone:+46 8 791 44 00

The Kungliga Operan or the Royal Swedish Opera hosts countless productions of theater, dance and music every year. Opening its door to the public in the late 1700s, the Kungliga Operan is Sweden's national stage. Even if you're not planning to see ballet or the opera during your stay in Stockholm, still make some time to visit the opera house and appreciate its lavishly ornate design. After all, it is big part of Stockholm and Sweden's culture and art.

Kungliga Operan Website
http://www.operan.se/
Kungliga Operan Map
https://goo.gl/maps/sMivfRf7Py12

Skansen Open-Air Museum

Location: Djurgårdsslätten 49-51, 115 21 Stockholm, Sweden
Opening Hours: Varies widely, see website for details (
Admission Fees: $7 to $21

Artur Hazelius founded Skansen, the first ever open-air museum in the world, in 1891. At Skansen, you will learn about the Swedish life through the centuries. You can also meet local Nordic animals, as well as enjoy annual festivities like St. Lucia's Day, which is held on December.

Skansen Open-Air Museum Website
http://www.skansen.se/en/kategori/english
Skansen Open-Air Museum Map
https://goo.gl/maps/bXpLcjzeJSU2

33

Must-Visit Museums

Art is an important part of any country or city's culture. Here are 5 museums in Stockholm you definitely should not miss. (Note: Museums listed in this chapter have free admissions unless noted otherwise.)

Medeltidsmuseet

Location: Strömparrterren 3, 111 30 Stockholm, Sweden
Opening Hours: 12:00 P.M. to 5:00 P.M. Tuesday, Thursday – Sunday
12:00 P.M. to 8:00 P.M. Wednesday

If you want to take a glimpse of Sweden's history, then you should visit the Medeltidsmuseet or the Medieval Museum in Stockholm. In their underground exhibition, you will find excavations of medieval town walls built in the 16th century. They also have an archaeological display of a market square, a church, and a council hall, all three of which are important parts of the country's medieval civilization.

Medeltidsmuseet Website
http://medeltidsmuseet.stockholm.se/in-english/
Medeltidsmuseet Map
https://goo.gl/maps/DXY449CDW8T2

Moderna Museet

Location: Exercisplan 4, Skeppsholmen, Stockholm, Sweden
Opening Hours: 10:00 A.M. to 8:00 P.M. Tuesday
10:00 A.M. to 6:00 P.M. Wednesday – Sunday

The Moderna Museet or the Modern Museum is probably the most famous museum in Stockholm. First opening its doors to the public in 1958, the Moderna Museet is home to contemporary artists who want to express their unique creativity.

Moderna Museet Website
http://www.modernamuseet.se/stockholm/en/
Moderna Museet Map
https://goo.gl/maps/ome9CmGGKs42

Nobel Museet

Location: Stortorget 2, 103 16 Stockholm, Sweden
Opening Hours: 9:00 A.M. to 8:00 P.M. Daily

The Nobel Museet was opened in 2001 as a center of knowledge and interest. It honors the life of Alfred Nobel, founder of the Nobel Prize, as well as the achievements of the Nobel Laureates. Its exhibitions range from science to art to design, and it even houses literary masterpieces such as that of Romanian-born German author Herta Müller.

Note: Free admission in the Nobel Museet is only on Tuesdays, from 5:00 P.M. to 8:00 P.M. Regular admission costs $12 for adults and $8 for students and senior citizens. Children up to 18 years old are admitted free.

Nobel Museet Website
http://www.nobelmuseum.se/
Nobel Museet Map
https://goo.gl/maps/Vdb5Ms5VvdT2

Vasa Museet

Location: Galärvarvsvägen 14, 115 21 Stockholm, Sweden
Opening Hours: June to August 8:30 A.M. to 6:00 P.M. Daily
September to May 10:00 A.M. to 5:00 P.M. Daily (except Wednesdays, 10:00 A.M. to 8:00 P.M.

Vasa was a real warship in the 17th century that sunk just minutes after leaving shore, and the Vasa Museet is where you can learn more about this historical catastrophe. There are exhibits detailing why Vasa was considered the great machine of war before it sank, what investigation followed the tragedy, and how the ship was salvaged so that it could continue to serve as a reminder of the country's past.

Note: Admission is only free for children up to 18 years old. The admission fee is $15.25 for adults and $12 for students.

Vasa Museet Website
http://www.vasamuseet.se/en
Vasa Museet Map
https://goo.gl/maps/gmBZ1R9VJRz

Arkitektur-och Designcentrum Skeppsholmen (ArkDes)

Location: Exercisplan 4, 111 49 Stockholm, Sweden
Opening Hours: 10:00 A.M. to 8:00 P.M. Tuesday
10:00 A.M. to 6:00 P.M. Wednesday – Sunday

Arkitektur-och Designcentrum Skeppsholmen, or ArkDes, is a national museum focusing on architecture and design. First founded in 1962, it exhibits the work of over 500 architects from all over Europe and the world. Its library is the home of more than 24 thousand books, and it archives architectural and design journals from the 1930s to the present time.

Arkitektur-och Designcentrum Skeppsholmen Website
http://www.arkdes.se/
Arkitektur-och Designcentrum Skeppsholmen Map
https://goo.gl/maps/K7cMDkSFik32

34

Must-Visit Art Galleries

If you still want to soak yourself with Swedish art and culture after visiting the museums from the last chapter, then these 5 art galleries are a must-visit for you.

Andréhn-Schiptjenko

Location: 2nd Floor, Hudiksvallsgatan 8, 113 30 Stockholm, Sweden
Opening Hours: 11:00 A.M. to 7:00 P.M. Thursday
11:00 A.M. to 4:00 P.M. Friday – Sunday
Admission Fees: None

Andréhn-Schiptjenko is a gallery that aims to influence future movements in art. With exhibitions from Scandinavian artists like Annika Larsson and Annika von Hausswolff, its growing popularity opened opportunities for bigger projects, including its participation in international art fairs in China, Mexico, and America. If you are in the mood for some contemporary art, then definitely pay Andréhn-Schiptjenko a visit during your stay in Stockholm.

Andréhn-Schiptjenko Website
http://www.andrehn-schiptjenko.com/
Andréhn-Schiptjenko Map
https://goo.gl/maps/aEjVUUvgr2u

Färgfabriken

Location: Lövholmsbrinken 1, 117 43 Stockholm, Sweden
Opening Hours: 11:00 A.M. to 6:00 P.M. Tuesday – Friday
12:00 P.M. to 4:00 P.M. Saturday
Admission Fees: $7 Regular Admission
$6 Students and Senior Citizens
Free for children up to 18 years old

Färgfabriken first opened in 1995, and it has since served as an art gallery for cultural and contemporary works of architecture, art, and urban design. Its main goal is to bring creativity from the world to Stockholm, and in effect, Färgfabriken to the rest of the world. Färgfabriken is the art gallery for people who want to immerse themselves in a global culture while visiting Stockholm. It is a good place to know how the city and Sweden react to globalization.

Färgfabriken Website
https://www.facebook.com/fargfabriken/
Färgfabriken Map
https://goo.gl/maps/Gpg7HfQhVn52

Fotografiska

Location: Stadsgårdshamnen 22, 116 45 Stockholm, Sweden
Opening Hours: 9:00 A.M. to 11:00 P.M. Sunday – Wednesday
9:00 A.M. to 1:00 A.M. Thursday – Saturday
Admission Fees: $14 Regular Admission
$10.50 Students and Senior Citizens
Free for children up to 12 years old

If photography is more up your alley, then Fotografiska is where you should go. This 2500-square-meter art gallery annually hosts 4 major and 15 to 20 minor exhibits. It features photographers from all over the world, and welcomes more than 500 thousand visitors each year. Because of the diversity of its artists, you should expect unique exhibitions that will not only entertain but will also arouse curiosity, creativity, and controversy. Fotografiska promises a worthwhile visit that will change your perspective of the world when you leave this art gallery.

Fotografiska Website
http://fotografiska.eu/en/
Fotografiska Map
https://goo.gl/maps/4JJnh4ECg7v

Galleri Charlotte Lund

Location: 6th Floor, Kungstensgatan 23, 113 57 Stockholm, Sweden
Opening Hours: 12:00 P.M. to 6:00 P.M. Tuesday – Friday
12:00 P.M. to 4:00 P.M. Saturday
Admission Fees: Currently not listed

Charlotte Lund founded the Galleri Charlotte Lund in 1993 with the purpose of opening visitors' eyes to the beauty and sophistication of contemporary art. This art gallery features established and upcoming Swedish artists at the same time. Unlike Fotografiska, Galleri Charlotte Lund is more rounded when it comes to the form of art. Here, you will find paintings, sketches, photographs, sculptures, videos, and installations that will all steer your creative mind.

Galleri Charlotte Lund Website
http://www.gallericharlottelund.com/
Galleri Charlotte Lund Map
https://goo.gl/maps/dBFma9XtPkn

Liljevalchs

Location: Djurgårdsvägen 60, 115 21 Stockholm, Sweden
Opening Hours: 11:00 A.M. to 5:00 P.M. Tuesday – Sunday
Admission Fees: Currently not listed on their website

Liljevalchs is the first ever independent contemporary art gallery in Sweden. First opened in 1916, this beautiful public museum was designed by architect Carl Bergsten, who intended to invite nature within its space. It hosts four major exhibitions every year, and it mostly features artists who specialize in contemporary and trendy forms of art and design.

Liljevalchs Website
https://www.facebook.com/liljevalchs/

Liljevalchs Map
https://goo.gl/maps/MbSEp1QhMHu

35

Best Coffee Shops

Aside from its rich art and history, Stockholm is best known for its coffee culture. Here in Stockholm, you will find numerous cafés that will satisfy your coffee craving. But to make your short travel a lot easier, this chapter has listed 5 of Stockholm's best coffee shops just for you. (Note: Price ranges listed on this chapter cover food items on the menu. Expect prices of coffee to be lower or within the range.)

Café Pascal

Location: 29C Östgötagatan, 116 25 Stockholm, Sweden
Opening Hours: 7:00 A.M. to 7:00 P.M. Monday – Thursday
7:00 A.M. to 6:00 P.M. Friday
9:00 A.M. to 6:00 P.M. Weekdays
Price Range: Currently not listed on their website

Rustic and industrial with a few modern touches, Café Pascal has a mid-century modern yet cozy ambiance that will make you feel at home. Its bright and airy space, as well as its good food and delicious coffee, make it one of the most visited coffee shops in Stockholm. Here, you can taste their signature bread and pastries while sipping a cup of their freshly brewed and slowly roasted fika. If you are looking for something to eat for lunch, you can also try their sandwiches and salads.

Café Pascal Website
http://cafepascal.se/
Café Pascal Map
https://goo.gl/maps/H1GKTjSUqC62

Coffice

Location: 29C Östgötagatan, 116 25 Stockholm, Sweden
Opening Hours: 7:45 A.M. to 6:00 P.M. Weekdays
10:00 A.M. to 6:00 P.M. Saturday
10:00 A.M. to 5:00 P.M. Saturday
Price Range: Currently not listed on their website

Coffice takes coffee ingenuity to heart. Opening its innovative space in 2009, Coffice (C from café and Office from office) is a place where people can work and enjoy coffee at the same time. The idea behind this coffee shop is to create an urban space to promote the working culture for those who are tired of working in the office or at home. In fact, customers can become members if they want to work at Coffice regularly, and they are given their own spaces in the coffee shop.

So if you have a few emails to send while in Stockholm, why don't you try visiting Coffice for a little cup of coffee? And even if you are planning to leave all work back at home, their delicious food, and drinks are still worth your time.

Coffice Website
http://coffice.coop/en/
Coffice Map
https://goo.gl/maps/vubi7Swkaj72

Drop Coffee

Location: Wollmar Yxkullsgatan 10, 118 50 Stockholm, Sweden
Opening Hours: 8:00 A.M. to 5:00 P.M. Weekdays
10:00 A.M. to 5:00 P.M. Weekends
Price Range: Currently not listed on their website

Joana Alm and Stephen Leighton, owners of Drop Coffee Café and Drop Coffee Roasters, are both experts in the art of roasting and brewing coffee. In their coffee shop, they serve their best coffee products, as well as lunch and breakfast items that were all well-crafted and thought-out. Alm and Leighton train their baristas to always achieve the perfect combination of acidity and sweetness in their coffee products. During your visit in Stockholm, stop by the Drop Coffee Café to taste their food and drinks, and maybe take home some of their wonderful coffee beans as well.

Drop Coffee Website
http://www.dropcoffee.com/
Drop Coffee Map
https://goo.gl/maps/PJd1PkopW642

Kafé Esaias

Location: Drottninggatan 102, 111 60 Stockholm, Sweden
Opening Hours: 7:30 A.M. to 5:00 P.M. Weekdays
10:00 A.M. to 5:00 P.M. Weekends
Price Range: $7.75 to $19

Kafé Esaias does not only serve delicious coffee; they have a full breakfast and lunch menu, too. Some of their breakfast items include sandwiches, granola, and sourdough, while their lunch menu includes a variety of salads and sandwiches. On weekends, they also serve a big brunch meal that will surely make your tummy happy. Kafé Esaias is popular for its warm and cozy ambience, and if you like to munch on some delicious comfort food during your visit in Stockholm, then give this coffee shop a try.

Kafé Esaias Website
https://www.facebook.com/kafeesaias/
Kafé Esaias Map
https://goo.gl/maps/a1UbHg67rxP2

Vete-Katten

Location: Kungsgatan 55, 111 22 Stockholm, Sweden
Opening Hours: 7:30 A.M. to 10:00 P.M. Weekdays
9:30 A.M. to 7:00 P.M. Weekends

Price Range: $9.25 to $14

Breakfast, salads, sandwiches, buns, biscuits, pastries, wine, tea, and coffee—Vete-Katten has it all. Famous for its freshly brewed cups of fika, the classic and elegant coffee shop will satisfy every craving you may ever have while in Stockholm. In fact, it is one of the most visited cafés in the city, and it has grown exponentially since Ester Nordhammar first opened it in 1928. Today, head chef Johan Sandelin continues to serve Vete-Katten's customers with good food and delicious drinks. His numerous awards, including Pastry Chef of the Year that he has won in 2002, can prove his talent in gastronomy.

Vete-Katten Website
http://www.vetekatten.se/en/
Vete-Katten Map
https://goo.gl/maps/zS67Kfx5mHD2

36

Nightlife—Best Bars

When you have seen the sights and have been soaked in the culture of Stockholm during the day, you might want to take a break from history lessons and try having some fun. In this chapter, you will find ways to enjoy the city's nightlife with these 5 awesome bars.

Erlands

Location: Gästrikegatan 1, 113 62 Stockholm, Sweden
Opening Hours: 5:00 P.M. to 11:00 P.M. Monday – Thursday
4:00 P.M. to 12:00 A.M. Friday – Saturday
Price Range: Drink prices currently not listed on their website

Erland opened only in 2013, yet its vintage design and ambience will take you back to the 1930s. This bar is a good place to have a drink and unwind. You can enjoy live performances while eating their delicious menu items and drinking their wide range of cocktails and other beverages.

Erlands Website
https://www.facebook.com/ErlandsCocktails/
Erlands Map
https://goo.gl/maps/MhxNX722mUA2

Häktet

Location: Hornsgatan 82, 118 21 Stockholm, Sweden
Opening Hours: 5:00 P.M. to 12:00 A.M. Monday – Tuesday
5:00 P.M. to 1:00 A.M. Wednesday
5:00 P.M. to 3:00 A.M. Thursday – Saturday
Price Range: $5.25 to $60 (for regular drinks)

In English, Häktet literally means detention, which makes sense as a name for this hip bar in Stockholm because it was built on the grounds where a jail was once erect. Nowadays, Häktet means good wine and liquor. With its white range of spirits, you will surely find something that suits your taste. The price of drinks start as low as $5.25, but the bar also sells the finest champagne, like the 1996 Vueve Clicquot Magnum Rose, which is priced at about $610.

Häktet also has a food menu that features delicious starters, main courses, and desserts. Starters begin at $3.50 (per oyster), main courses begin at $26.50, and desserts begin at $6.50.

Häktet Website
https://www.facebook.com/haktet/
Häktet Map
https://goo.gl/maps/NRBfSgoowP72

Pharmarium

Location: Stortorget 7, 111 29 Stockholm, Sweden
Opening Hours: 6:00 P.M. to 2:00 A.M. Wednesday – Saturday
Price Range: $16.50 to $18.25

Inspired by the first pharmacy built in the city, Pharmarium gets a little scientific when making its drinks. It has concoctions like Tea + Therapy, where they combine different types of tea with Hendrick's gin. At Pharmarium, your palette will have a wonderful time experimenting with exotic combinations of liquor and other ingredients.

Pharmarium Website
http://pharmarium.se/
Pharmarium Map
https://goo.gl/maps/63pMUnsUsE22

Restaurang Aktiebolaget Kvarnen

Location: Tjärhovsgatan 4, 116 21 Stockholm, Sweden
Opening Hours: 11:00 A.M. to 1:00 A.M. Monday – Tuesday
11:00 A.M. to 3:00 A.M. Wednesday to Friday
12:00 P.M. to 3:00 A.M. Saturday
12:00 P.M. to 1:00 A.M. Sunday
Price Range: $6.50 to $23.35 (for regular drinks)

Restaurang Aktiebolaget Kvarnen, or simply Kvarnen, is one of the most popular bars in Stockholm. It has a tavern theme that pays homage to the year when it first opened, back in 1908. The atmosphere here is warm and lively, and it takes you back to the farmstead life that people lived in Sweden all those years ago. Kvarnen has many drink options, but its bestseller is the classic beer. You should also try their food and wine.

Restaurang Aktiebolaget Kvarnen Website
https://www.facebook.com/kvarnen.hospodske.dveri/
Restaurang Aktiebolaget Kvarnen Map
https://goo.gl/maps/ewoYdXCjnFn

Tweed

Location: Lilla Nygatan 5, 111 28 Stockholm, Sweden
Opening Hours: 5:00 P.M. to 12:00 A.M. Monday – Thursday
3:00 P.M. to 1:00 A.M. Friday
5:00 P.M. to 1:00 A.M. Saturday
Price Range: Currently not listed on the website

All aboard!—Tweed has a nautical theme that goes along well with their liquor and other alcohol products. Here at Tweed, you can have a nice drink, smoke a good Cuban, and eat some delicious food—just like the sailors back in the day did. Moreover, they sometimes have live performances that you can enjoy during your visit. Their snacks are priced as low as $4, while their main course items start at $20.56.

Tweed Website
http://start.leijontornet.se/
Tweed Map
https://goo.gl/maps/HZSfj3dAiuH2

37

Nightlife—Best Nightclubs

If drinking and dancing are more your thing, then a simple bar might not be enough. Here are 5 of the best places to dance the night away in Stockholm:

Göta Källare

Location: Folkungagatan 45, 118 26 Stockholm, Sweden
Opening Hours: 10:00 P.M. to 3:00 A.M. Wednesday, Friday – Saturday

If one dance floor isn't enough for you, then check out Göta Källare and its 2 dance floors. Divided into 2 levels, its almost 4000-square-foot dance floor is enough space for everyone to enjoy their techno beats and futuristic sounds. They have live DJs performing, so you know you will have a good time.

Göta Källare Website
http://gotakallare.com/site/
Göta Källare Map
https://goo.gl/maps/JgkjoGKKrcK2

Kåken

Location: Regeringsgatan 66, 111 39 Stockholm, Sweden
Opening Hours: 5:00 A.M. to 11:00 P.M. Monday – Thursday
4:00 A.M. to 12:00 A.M. Friday – Saturday

Kåken suits the more elegant and classy crowd. Its vintage interior will definitely bring you back to the 20s and 30s, but you will still have a really good time hanging out in this club.

Kåken Website
https://www.facebook.com/kakensthlm
Kåken Map
https://goo.gl/maps/5TpbGAYC1Bm

Restaurang Solidaritet

Location: Lästmakargatan 3, 111 44 Stockholm, Sweden

Opening Hours: 11:00 P.M. to 5:00 A.M. Wednesday – Saturday

Modern, trendy and fun—those are just some of the words that describe Restaurang Solidaritet. Aside from its crowded and energetic dance floor, and its great music from Swedish and international DJs, this club also has a refreshing menu of drinks that you will surely love.

Restaurang Solidaritet Website
https://www.facebook.com/SLDRTT/
Restaurang Solidaritet Map
https://goo.gl/maps/YZt3QFCTAPM2

Södra Bar

Location: Mosebacke Torg 1, 116 46 Stockholm
Opening Hours: 5:00 A.M. to 11:00 P.M. Monday – Thursday
4:00 A.M. to 12:00 A.M. Friday – Saturday

Another place with good drinks and great live acts is the Södra Bar. Its ornate interior design, which is inspired by the Kungliga Operan, adds to that elegant and royal feel of the club. When you get a little tired on the dance floor, you can also take a moment to relax at their beautiful open-air veranda. Have a couple drinks, sit back, and enjoy the view of Stockholm.

Södra Bar Website
https://www.facebook.com/SodraTeatern/
Södra Bar Map
https://goo.gl/maps/NQAiY436w742

Stampen

Location: Stora Nygatan 5, 111 27 Stockholm, Sweden
Opening Hours: 5:00 P.M. to 1:00 A.M. Tuesday – Friday
2:00 P.M. to 1:00 A.M. Saturday

If techno beats are not your thing and you just want some live jazz music to get your body dancing, then Stampen is the place for you. Its live jazz music with its good food, good beer, and good wine will definitely give you a great time.

Stampen Website
https://www.facebook.com/stampen.se/
Stampen Map
https://goo.gl/maps/X6JNsBzjR2x

38

Special Must-Try Activities

ABBA: The Museum & Swedish Music Hall of Fame

Location: Strömparrterren 3, 111 30 Stockholm, Sweden
Opening Hours: Varies widely, see website for details.
Phone:+46 8 121 328 60

Abba was a Swedish pop group that was responsible for international hits like Dancing Queen, Mamma Mia, Take a Chance on Me, and The Winner Takes It All, all of which are now a part of the popular musical Mamma Mia's soundtrack. If you want to discover the roots and the progression of Abba to global stardom, then you should pay ABBA: The Museum & Swedish Music Hall of Fame a visit while in Stockholm.

The Museum & Swedish Music Hall of Fame
http://www.abbathemuseum.com/en/groups-and-events-0
The Museum & Swedish Music Hall of Fame
https://goo.gl/maps/akTz28iVmvu

Boat Sightseeing

You have two options if you want to go sightseeing by boat in Stockholm. One, you can go with Strömma, where you have the chance to cruise under bridges of Stockholm while enjoying the views of the city.The other option is by Red, where you get to tour under 17 bridges in an hour and 45 minutes. You will also be taken to where the Baltic Sean and Lake Mälaren connect. Both sightseeing options also offer bus tours.

Phone:+46 8 120 040 00
Boat Sightseeing Website
http://www.stromma.se/en/stockholm/
sightseeing/sightseeing-by-boat/
Boat Sightseeing Map
https://goo.gl/maps/qb2wTPhBRuL2

Rooftop Hiking

Yes, hiking on a rooftop is another activity that you can do in Stockholm. For only $70, you can tour around Stockholm from a different view—the roofs. You can take pictures of the city skyline, unobstructed by the bustling streets down low. And even though selfie sticks are not allowed on this tour, guides are nice enough to take your group pictures for you.

Phone:+46 8 22 30 05

Rooftop Hiking Website
https://www.takvandring.com/en/home
Rooftop Hiking Map
https://goo.gl/maps/YKtwf8LnUzz

SkyView

Location: Ericsson Globen, Globentorget 2, Stockholm, Sweden
Opening Hours: 9:30 A.M. to 6:00 P.M. Weekdays
9:30 A.M. to 4:00 P.M. Weekends

In SkyView, you will have the chance to reach the peak of the world's largest spherical building. At 425 feet above sea level, you will also have the best view of Sweden's beautiful city.

Phone:+46 77 181 10 00
SkyView Website
http://www.globearenas.se/skyview/om-skyview
SkyView Map
https://goo.gl/maps/CY4UzBXxSpR2

Winter Activities

Stockholm is also beautiful during the winter. There are a lot of activities that you can do including 1) getting a room in one of their 200 ski resorts, 2) tracking some wolves, reindeers and bears on a safari, 3) spending a night in an actual igloo, 4) driving a dog sled, 5) catching fish from a frozen lake, 6) riding a snowmobile on a frozen river, and lastly, 7) seeing the majestic Northern Lights in the sky.

Ski Stockholm Website
https://www.skistar.com/en/Hammarbybacken/
About-Hammarbybacken/
Ski Stockholm Map
https://goo.gl/maps/5VPB7iJQDcv
Phone:+46 8 641 68 30

Safari Website
http://www.wildsweden.com/
Safari Map
https://goo.gl/maps/pq5AXbdoGjH2
Phone:+46 70 610 61 50

Igloo Website (ice hotel)
http://www.icehotel.com/about-icehotel/
Ice Bar Website
http://www.icebarstockholm.se/en/
Ice Bar Map
https://goo.gl/maps/dFQ4JYPKFjy
Phone:+46 8 505 635 20

Dog Sledding Website
http://dogsleddinginsweden.com/
Phone:+46 644 700 06

Fishing Sweden Website
http://www.fishing-in-sweden.com/

Sweden Adventures Website
https://www.whitetrailadventures.com/

Phone:+46 (0)730 469 304

Northern Lights Sweden Website
https://www.theaurorazone.com/destinations/
northern-lights-holidays-to-sweden
Phone:01670 785012

39

Travel Safety Tips

Have you booked a trip to Stockholm yet? Before you leave for a vacation to this foreign city, make sure to follow these travel safety tips in order to keep you and your belongings safe during your holiday.

Make copies of your passport and bring a couple with you when you travel. If your real passport gets lost or is stolen, you still need something to prove your citizenship. Also, leave a copy of your passport back home, either in your residence or with a trusted friend. It will also help if you have a digital copy of your passport in your mobile device and/or email.

See your doctor and ask if you need to get shots before you leave. For the trip, you should also ask for a prescription of your regular medications, if you are taking any.

Check-in with your medical insurance to see if it applies for international travel. If not, it is advisable to get additional insurance for your trip.

Find out what the exchange rate is beforehand. As of writing this book, a Swedish Krona is equal to 12 cents in the US Dollar. It is important that you have an idea of what the exchange rate is so you won't be ripped off when you convert your money. Also, a bank or an ATM will be your best option for exchanging currency. Most conversion centers apply additional fees.

Exchange Rate Website
http://www.xe.com/currencyconverter/

Call your bank before you leave and inform them that you are traveling. In the middle of your vacation, your credit card provider might turn off your card without warning, thinking that your transactions are fraud. It is also wise to call your provider to ask if your credit card will work overseas.

Lastly, inform a friend or family member about your trip. Leave them with your departure and arrival details, as well as your itinerary for your entire trip. In the case of an emergency, they will know which hotel to call and where you are supposed to be going while you are away.

40

Three-Day Itinerary

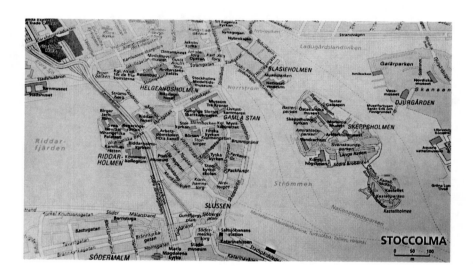

Day 1: History and Culture

Check-in at your hotel and immediately tour around the city. Start with a boat sightseeing tour of Stockholm's historical landmarks such as the City Hall, the Royal Palace, and Gamla Stan.

After the boat sightseeing tour, you can travel by bus or train to Medeltidsmuseet or the Vasa Museet to get a better sense of Stockholm's colorful history. In the evening, you can then unwind by buying a couple drinks at one of Stockholm's bars that were listed on this book.

Day 2: Food and Arts

You can spend day 2 by going on a culinary trip around the city. Take a tour around the city's cafés and taste their delicious cups of fika. Eat at some of the restaurants listed on this travel guide as well. You can also find street vendors selling food in carts.

While on this culinary adventure, why don't you also take a trip around the museums and art galleries listed on this book? Be amazed by the beauty in pictures at Fotografiska, appreciate contemporary and modern art over at Medeltidsmuseet, and get astonished by the innovative and inventive lives of the Nobel Laureates over at the Nobel Museet.

If you're still energized to do something in the nighttime, go dancing at one of the nightclubs listed on this book. There's no better way to end the evening than with a couple of delicious drinks, some good music, and a crowded dance floor to keep you company.

Day 3: Other Activities

Day 3 is the day to just enjoy the city and soak in its beauty. Visit a park and appreciate the greenery of the city, or have some fun by doing any of the activities listed on Chapter 12. Before you leave Stockholm, make sure to take a lot of pictures of its beautiful architecture and historical landscape so you have something to remember your trip by.

41

HELSINKI INTRODUCTION

So You're Going to **Helsinki?**

"Tervetuloa"

That's the Finnish translation of the English word "welcome."

Once you step foot in Helsinki, Finland's capital city, that's a word you'll probably hear often. Since the Finns are typically accommodating and hospitable, having an awkward introductory experience is unlikely. They'll shake your hand, and they might even ask you whether you want them to show you around.

There, a glorious batch of interesting people, historical landmarks, one-of-a-kind attractions, unique traditions, art galleries, night-clubs, and other exciting things are waiting for you!

If you're after an outrageous journey, it's the ideal place for you. So why not check it out?

Make sure to have enough money (in euros) with you. Have plans in place and you're good to go!

42

Helsinki Then & Now

When you approach a local in Helsinki about your location, don't be surprised if he tells you "you're in this (____) part of Hessa" or "you're in this part of Stadi".

You might freak out for a bit. But, learn to keep it cool. You're still in Helsinki.

The slang words for Helsinki are Hessa and Stadi. Many locals use these informal terms frequently.

Moreover, the words Hessa and Stadi are but two in the lineup of uncommon things about the capital city. Because Helsinki has been an (unofficial) residence since the 14th century, it's very rich in history. Definitely, there's still plenty of information about it worth discovering.

A Brief History

The founder of Helsinki is Sweden's King Gustavus Vasa. He founded the Russian-dependent city on December 6, 1550. It began with the reputation as the competitor city of Estonia's Tallinn and as Southern Finland's new trading port.

In 1812, Helsinki was recognized officially as a progressive city. It was also then that Helsinki became Finland's capital.

From then on, developments began. It soon became an industrial and an administrative place. It started to make way for economic and political growth.

Facts about the city during the early days:

- Helsinki had a strong reputation. Despite the unforgettable marks of the Finnish Winter War and the Finnish Civil War, it thrived.
- The original city name is Helsingfors (in Swedish) and Gelsingfors (in Russian).
- To reduce the Swedish influence on Helsinki's people, The Royal Academy of Turku (Russia's 1st university), was relocated to Finland's capital city.

Location, Population & Geography

-Helsinki is located in the southern part of Finland, on the Gulf of

Finland's shore and in the Uusimaa region. To the east is Stockholm, Sweden (400 km). To the west is Saint Petersburg, Russia (388 km). To the North is Tallinn, Estonia (80 km).

As of 2016, Helsinki has a city population of more than 600,000 and an urban population of more than 1,100,000. The city has a majority of bilingual speakers since Finland is officially bilingual. 84% of the population speaks Finnish, 6% speaks Swedish, and the remaining 10% speaks a mix of English and other languages.

Daughter of the Baltic is Helsinki's other name. The particular name acknowledges its location at the peninsula's tip. It's surrounded by more than 300 islands. The major islands are Korkeasaari, Lauttasaari, Seurasaari, and Vallisaari.

The Capital Region & the Metropolis

Helsinki's Capital Region consists of four municipalities. These municipalities are Espoo, Helsinki, Kaunianen, and Vantaa. It has a high housing density since 0.2% of its surface area is allotted for 20% of Finland's total population.

Meanwhile, Helsinki's Metropolitan Area (or the Greater Helsinki region) is the northernmost area in the world. It consists of 11 surrounding municipalities. It covers an area of more than 3, 600 km2. As of 2016, you can find an estimation of ¼ of Finland's total population in the Metropolitan Area.

Maintaining a 1st Class Reputation

In 1995, when Finland became a part of the European Union, growth was achieved. Helsinki was recognized as a center for educational, financial, economic, and political affairs. As of 2016, more than 70% of major companies operating in Finland are located in the capital city.

Helsinki has continued to progress through the years. Because of its impressive reputation, it has garnered major recognitions. Two of these are: (1) it was included in the Livable Cities Index 2011, according to Monocle and (2) it was in the top 10 of the best cities worldwide, according to the Economist's Intelligence Unit.

43

When Is the Best Time to Visit Helsinki?

There's this phenomenon called The Midnight Sun.

It's a natural occurrence during the summer solstice. It shows the sun's availability during midnight. Because of its splendid sight, it offers a relaxing view.

Astronomers of all levels and travelers are among the bunch who call themselves fans of the natural phenomenon. You might want to be one of them, too. After all, you might not get to see the sun during midnight.

Where's a perfect place to catch The Midnight Sun, you ask?

You can witness the phenomenon in territories where the Arctic Circle crosses. One of these territories is Helsinki!

Hot Summer Days

June, July, and August are the hot summer months in Helsinki. These are said to be the best months to visit Helsinki because the sun is out during these months. According to many travelers, you can appreciate the wonderful city during this time of the year.

Usually, the temperature doesn't go above 50 degrees during summer in Helsinki. The warmth is tolerable. Somehow, it encourages you to wander around the city with a bright mood. This is one reason why travelers flock the city during these months.

Tips on visiting Helsinki during summer:
- Be ready with raincoats for you and for your belongings; though it rarely rains, it's best to have these things handy
- Carry a bottle of water
- Wear a hat
- Wear proper attire; wear a comfortable shirt and jeans
- Wear sunglasses

Best summer activities in Helsinki:
- Attend The Midsummer Eve on June 24; it's a celebration that involves handicraft demonstrations, bonfires, folk dancing, music, spells, and a variety of games
- Attend The Taste of Helsinki; it's a culinary festival that occurs from June 16 to 19
- Check out the open-air markets
- Go on a boat tour; explore the islands
- Enjoy crayfish season; it occurs around July
- Strolling around the city streets
- Watch street performances

What's Winter Like?

Winter in Finland occurs during the months of December, January, and February. You can join other travelers who retreat to Helsinki during winter. But, take note that when you are longing for outdoor activities under the sun, winter days might not be the days for you.

In Helsinki, compared to the other parts of Finland, the winter days are notably warmer. It's rare for temperatures to drop below -4F(-20 celsius). Nevertheless, it's cold in the city. If you're inexperienced when it comes to snow, snow-covered streets and homes, and conditions below the freezing point, the place may be a shocker – unless, of course, you prepare.

Another possible shocker? During most winter days, the average day doesn't last long. After about five hours and forty-eight minutes, the sun begins to let darkness, along with cloudy weather, take charge. It can seem a bit odd for foreigners. For locals, though, it's not.

Tips on visiting Helsinki during winter:
- Be ready with rain coats (for you and for your belongings)
- Wear the proper attire; wear a sweater, a pair (and more) of thermal socks, mittens, layer of clothes, gloves, and scarf
- When traveling by car, make sure to have studded, winter tires

Best winter activities in Helsinki:

- Go dog sledding
- Go ice breaker sailing
- Go ice fishing
- Go skiing
- Ride a snowmobile
- Stay in an igloo
- Watch a local hockey match
- Watch the northern lights

44

What You Need to Know about Transportation

The Helsinki Airport: Offering Excellent Service

The Helsinki Airport (HEL) is an international airport. It's located 17 km north of the Helsinki City Center, in Vantaa. It's operator is Finnavia and it serves as a hub for different air carriers.

Helsinki Airport Website
http://www.finavia.fi/en/helsinki-airport/
Helsinki Airport Map
https://goo.gl/maps/bUgF58GRjoq

Getting Into Helsinki

You can get into Helsinki by train, bus or taxi.

Helsinki Airport Transport Website
http://www.finavia.fi/en/helsinki-airport/
to-and-from/train-buses-and-taxis/
Helsinki Airport Rail Website
https://www.hsl.fi/en/timetables-and-routes/
terminals/transport-links-helsinki-airport

Some air carriers in the Helsinki Airport:

- Nordic Regional Airlines
- TUlfly Nordic
- Jet Time
- Freebird Airlines
- Scandinavian Airlines
- Norwegian Air Shuttle

According to statistics, the Helsinki Airport holds an outstanding record. Annually, it serves more than 2,000,000 domestic passengers. It also serves more than 13,000,000 international passengers.

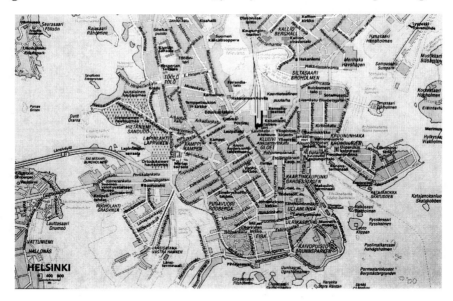

Destinations:

- Bangkok
- Beijing

- Brussels
- Cincinnati
- Dubai
- Frankfurt
- Hong Kong
- Istanbul
- London
- Mariehamn
- Moscow
- New York
- Osaka
- Paris
- St. Petersburg

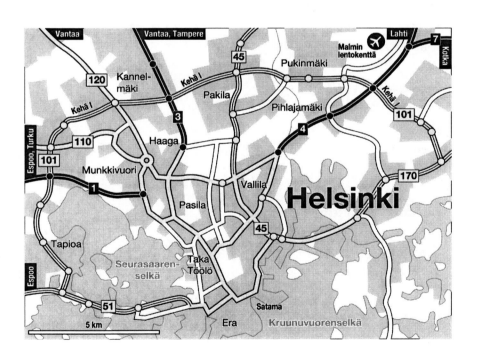

Transport in Helsinki

Helsinki Street Map
https://goo.gl/maps/a8uUZKrzMJ52

Did you know that Helsinki is Finland's only city with subways and trams?

Helsinki features The Helsinki Metro. It's a rapid transit system under the operations of HKL (or Helsinki City Transport) for HSL (or Helsinki Transport Authority). After twenty-seven years of planning, it opened to the public on August 2, 1982.

Annually, it carries an estimated 62,000,000 passengers. It has two lines (M1: Vuosaari to Matinkylä and M2: Mellunmäki to Tapiola). Since its availability, as well as its accessibility, is impressive, why not use it as a means to navigate the city?

Helsinki Metro Website 1
http://www.hel.fi/www/hkl/en/by-metro/
Helsinki Metro Website 2
https://www.hsl.fi/en/timetables-and-routes/
routemaps

Options for Getting by

Under the HSL's management, Helsinki public transport covers transportation within Helsinki. You can now easily wander around the city and hop on to nearby regions. Among these nearby regions are Espoo, Kerava, Kirkkonummi, Sipoo, and Vantaa.

Since it first opened in the 1980s, Helsinki public transport is responsible of 50% of commuting services within Helsinki. This suggests that more than half of the population is satisfied with the system.

Public Transport Website
http://www.hel.fi/www/hkl/en/by-tram/
Public Transport Website 2
https://www.hsl.fi/en/timetables-and-routes
Public Transport Website 3
https://www.facebook.com
/helsinginseudunliikenne

Public Transport Phone :09 4766 4000
- **Bus**

Since the buses in Helsinki are designated in chief points within the city, you're unlikely to have trouble getting around when you're sight-seeing. These buses are assigned to follow many routes and most of them stop at major attractions.

A tip? Hang out at the city center; there, the buses pass by regularly. You won't have to wait long when you're searching for one, too. In most cases, less than 10 minutes is all it takes.

Bus Website
https://www.hsl.fi/en

Types of buses:

-Regional buses
-Regular buses

Route variants:
- A-variant – refers to a clockwise or lengthened route
- B-variant – refers to a counter-clockwise or shortened route
- K-variant – refers to an exception in the route

- N-variant – refers to nighttime lines (with operations between 23:30 and 1:30)
- T-variant – refers to trams to terminals
- V-variant – refers to the more direct route
- Z-variant – refers to the more direct way (along the highway)

-Trunk bus services
- **City bikes**

Another option for getting by is by going through the Banaa in Helsinki.

The Banaa is a term that refers to a lane especially for pedestrians and bicyclists. It is a 1200-km formation of bike paths. It has won the hearts of pedestrians and cyclists, as well as dog-walkers, joggers, and skateboarders.

With the Banaa and Helsinki's bike system, you can explore the different amazing points around the city by riding a bike. You also have the option to access parks, harbors, forests, and quiet fields. As of May 2016, the city features 50 bike hubs and 500 bikes that serve the city area.

Moreover, you can also avail of biking tours that private companies in Helsinki offer. It entails additional fun if you bike with a bunch of people. In fact, cycling groups aren't rare.

City Bicycle Website
https://www.hsl.fi/en/citybikes
Bicycle Rental Website
http://www.bicycleanhelsinki.com/
Bicycle Map
https://goo.gl/maps/dghaGNowW9J2

· **Commuter train**

Trains are another cool way to get around Helsinki. That's according to the record of more than 800 departures on weekdays.

Commuter trains allow you to unravel the northeast and northwest regions in downtown Helsinki. It consists of 14 separate services and it runs on all the branches that start at the Helsinki Central Railway Station. Chiefly, it operates above the ground within the major areas of the city.

Helsinki Central Railway Station Map
https://goo.gl/maps/BuHLFb5xTW82

Commuter train routes:
· Line A – operates from Helsinki to Leppävaara
· Line E – operates from Helsinki to Kauklahti
· Line L – operates from Helsinki to Kirkkonummi (runs nightly and on weekday mornings)
· Line U – operates from Helsinki to Kirkkonummi (runs twice hourly)
· Line X – operates from Helsinki to Kirkkonummi
· Line Y – operates from Helsinki to Siuntio
· The Ring Rail Line – operates from Helsinki to Tikkurila
· Train D – operates from Helsinki to Riihimäki (runs as a rush hour service)

- Train K – operates from Helsinki to Kerava (runs once)
- Train N – operates from Helsinki to Kerava (runs early morning and late night)
- Train R – operates from Helsinki to Riihimäki (runs twice daily)
- Train T – operates from Helsinki to Riihimäki (runs once nightly)
- Train Z – operates from Helsinki to Lahti

Train Website
https://www.vr.fi/cs/vr/en/commuter_service_timetables
Public Transport Website
https://www.hsl.fi/en/information/how-use-public-transport

- **Ferry**

A ferryboat in Helsinki serves as another great option.

Helsinki is proud of its two ferry lines. Suomenlinnan Liikenne Oy is the operator of both lines. The ferries establish a connection to an emergency vehicle tunnel.

<u>Two ferry lines:</u>
- Mainland to Korkeasaari Zoo
- Mainland Soumenlinna

Moreover, due to Helsinki's location on the Baltic Sea, the Helsinki ferry port is a gateway to different European regions. Since it was founded in 1550, it continually provides transportation to countries such as Estonia, Russia, and Sweden. It has numerous ferry terminals. The trips have long sailing times of up to seventeen hours.

Ferry Website 1
http://www.hel.fi/www/helsinki/en/maps-and-transport/transport/ferry/water-transport/water-transport
Ferry Website 2
http://www.aferry.com/helsinki-ferry.htm

- <u>**Tram**</u>

Since the 1900s, the Helsinki tram system has operated continuously. The trams run based on a network that consists of (almost) double tracks. These are powered from overhead wires.

Most of the tramways in Helsinki are situated on the street – on dedicated tram lanes. Trams have their separate traffic lights to make them distinguishable from normal streetlights. According to HELMI (or Helsinki Public Transport Signal Priority & Passenger Information), the synchronization allows buses and trams to flow smoothly.

Streetlight symbols of trams:
- Horizontal line – means prepare to stop
- Letter S – means stop
- Upward-pointing arrow – means go

Tram Website
http://www.hel.fi/www/hkl/en/by-tram/

45

HOTELS :Best Affordable & Quality Hotels

Do you want a mystical experience?

Do you want to be accommodated with uncomplicated service?
Do you want to stay in unique designer rooms?

Do you want a passionate, emotional experience with one-of-a-kind interiors?

Do you want modern and edgy themes?

If you want all these amazing things, consider checking in at **Klaus K**.

The Klaus K

The Klaus K is Helsinki's 1st design hotel. Kalevala, the national epic, inspired its design. Since it's in the heart of the city, it provides easy access to a truckload of attractions.

Klaus K Website
http://www.klauskhotel.com/en/
Klaus K Map
https://goo.gl/maps/irCUoYBMz3p
Address
-Bulevardi 2, 00120 Helsinki, Finland
Tel:+358 20 7704700

Helsinki's Affordable & Excellent Hotel Options

Because the city was named as the World Design Capital, you can expect a wonderful time when you're in Helsinki. At almost every corner, every street, and every building you look at, you'd be swooned. Among these awesome establishments in the place are the hotels.

You don't have to worry too much about the costs. The rates are reasonable.

If you're travelling with a tight budget, you'd be delighted to know that there's a ton of excellent options for you.

Top five options:

Ava Hotel

Ava Hotel is one of Helsinki's popular hotels because of its convenient location near the city center. If you wish to spend most of your time roaming around the city, write down this hotel's name and address on your list.

Star rating: 3 stars
Address: 6 Karstulantie, Keskinen Suurpiiri
Room types: -Two-bedroom apartment
-Three-bedroom apartment
-Standard twin room
-Studio apartment
Facilities: Gym
Fitness center
Sauna
Rates: Around 49 € per night (for one person)
Ava Hotel Website
http://www.ava.fi/hotel-ava
Ava Hotel Map
https://goo.gl/maps/EtEJXARbSGq
Tel:+358 9 774751

Cumulus Kallio

Near the heart of the city is the cozy hotel, Cumulus Kallio. Once you've experience Helsinki's attractions, an extra comfortable room is waiting for you.

Star rating: 3 stars
Address: 2 Läntinen Brahenkatu, Keskinen Suurpiiri

Room types: -Standard single room
-Standard twin room
-Superior double room
-Superior triple room

Facilities: Bowling alley
Cycling station
Gym
Sauna
Swimming pool
Rates: Around 150 € per night (for one person)

Cumulus Kallio Website
https://www.cumulus.fi/en/hotels/cumulus-kallio-helsinki
Cumulus Kallio Map
https://goo.gl/maps/W5RDhCbq2vD2
Tel:+358 200 48109

Dommus Academia

Are you interested in staying at an eco-friendly place in Helsinki?
Dommus Academia is the hotel to check into! If you don't want
any trouble when hopping from the hotel to other parts of the city,
you won't regret your stay. A bus and metro stations are just five
minutes away from the location.

Star rating: 3 stars
Address: 14 Hietaniemenkatu, Eteläinen Suurpiiri
Room types: -Single room
-Twin room
-Triple room
-Bunk bed (male dormitory)
-Bunk bed (female dormitory)

-Economy single room
-Economy twin room

<u>Facilities</u>: Gift shop
Restaurant
Sauna
Rates: Around 40 € per night (for one person)
Dommus Academia Website
http://www.hostelacademica.fi/
Dommus Academia Map
https://goo.gl/maps/BtsGk0Dd6R92
<u>Tel:</u>+358 9 13114334

Forenom Merihaka

If you start your day with a cup of coffee, the coffee maker inside your room at Forenom Merihaka will set you in a great mood when exploring Helsinki. You can then head to the nearby cathedral and music center for vibes that are more positive.

<u>Star rating</u>: 2 stars
<u>Address</u>: 7 to 9 Haapaniemenkatu, Keskinen Suurpiiri
<u>Room types</u>: -Single room w/ shared bathroom
-Double room w/ shared bathroom
<u>Rates</u>: Around 50 € per night (for one person)

Forenom Merihaka Website
http://forenom.fi/en/hostels/helsinki-merihaka/
Forenom Merihaka Map
https://goo.gl/maps/ehtajTnTNhM2
<u>Tel:</u>+358 20 1983420

Omena Hotel

Because the Helsinki Central Station is just around the corner, consider Omena Hotel. It's a fine hotel for a brief stay in Helsinki. The interiors are quite basic, but they make way for a relaxing scene. Staying at this place is a great idea for two reasons: it's near the central station and the rates are reasonable.

Star rating: 3 stars
Address: 13 Lönnrotinkatu, Eteläinen Suurpiiri
Room types: –Single room
–Double room
–Family room
Rates: 49 € per night (for one person)

Omena Hotel Website
https://www.omenahotels.com/en/hotels/helsinki-lonnrotinkatu-en/
Omena Hotel Map
https://goo.gl/maps/DV5cUjF8FCM2
Tel:+358 600 555222

46

Let's Eat: Best Restaurants in Helsinki

One famous delicacy in Helsinki is **perunarieska**.

Perunaieska is potato flat bread. Its main ingredients are potatoes, barley flour, and eggs.

It became a top delicacy in Helsinki because of the harsh climate during most days of the year. The regular unavailability of fresh fruits and vegetables made the locals highly reliant on potato (among many staple tubers).

Nowadays, people in Helsinki add extra excitement to their signature flavors. Before, it was more about stable tubers. Well, long gone are those days.

Excellent Restaurants around Helsinki

All around Helsinki, finding a retreat to satisfy a hungry stomach is effortless. Along most streets are lineups of snack bars and restaurants.

As the locals would advise, if you want to try the best salivating flavors of Helsinki meals, make sure to stop by at particular restaurants. Whether you're on the lookout for Finnish delicacies or you want a dish of international favorites, the finest should be the ones worth checking out.

Top five restaurants:

– Chef & Sommelier

Looking for organic delicacies? Looking for sumptuous meals?
If so, Chef & Sommelier is the place to go. It's located within walking distance from the city center. Because of its healthy European and Scandinavian themes, it's a favorite of the locals. According to the locals, the food, along with its service, is excellence personified.

Menu includes:
Buckwheat and ransom

Cabbage and beans
Carrot and pine
Cucumber and sour milk
Lapland cow
Meadowsweet
Rhubarb and rose
Whitefish and herbs

Chef & Sommelier Website
http://chefetsommelier.fi/en/
Chef & Sommelier Map
https://goo.gl/maps/372g7itfTaK2
Phone :+358 40 0959440
Address: Huvilakatu 28, 00150 Helsinki

– Juuri

For a glorious serving of Finnish flavors and a selection of unique beers, Juuri is the restaurant to dine in. Especially if you're quite restless from city tours, the place won't disappoint. According to reviews, the setting is splendid!

Menu includes:
Grilled beef with cauliflower
Salt caramel cake
Cucumber soup
Organic egg with mushrooms
Whitefish with horseradish and elderflower
Quark with marjoram

Juuri Website
http://juuri.fi/en/
Juuri Map

https://goo.gl/maps/55mvwtvFwJs
Phone :+358 9 635732
Address: Korkeavuorenkatu 27, 00130 Helsinki

- Nokka

At Nokka, the meals are nothing short of appetizing. As the locals put it, everything in the menu is well crafted. The foods are delicious, the choice of wines is excellent, and the overall presentation is impressive.

To top it off, Nokka is situated in a fascinating setting. It's located is in a traditional building with awesome interiors. It boasts of wonderful views, as well.

Menu includes:
Rhubarb and quinces
Air-dried asparagus
Domestic cheese
Nokka Website
http://www.ravintolanokka.fi/en/front-page/
Nokka Map
https://goo.gl/maps/k4L3ibwszQ62
Phone :+358 9 61285600
Address: F, Kanavaranta 7, 00160 Helsinki

- Ragu

Ragu serves Central European, European, and Scandinavian de-lights to everyone in Helsinki. If you're craving for those kinds of flavors, your next destination should be at this restaurant. According to the locals, it's as if you can't admire the place enough. The foods and drinks were spectacular!

Menu includes:
Cockerel breast and liver
Organic lamb sirloin and neck
Shellfish
Pike Wallenberg with potato
Ragu Website
http://www.ragu.fi/
Ragu Map
https://goo.gl/maps/FEJsvJqhtxQ2
Phone :+358 9 596659
Address:Ludvigsgatan 3, 00130 Helsinki

– Ravintola Tokyo55

If you're hungry for sushi and other Japanese and Asian favorites, head to Ravintola Tokyo55. It has flavorful meals and cool cocktails.

Ravintola Tokyo55's location is quite far from Helsinki's city center. While some are not pleased, other people are fine with it being off the city. For those who prefer a quiet setting, it serves as the ideal place.

Menu includes:
Scampi
Miso soup
Green tea ice cream
Duck liver

Ravintola Tokyo55 Website
http://tokyo55.fi/menu/
Ravintola Tokyo55 Map
https://goo.gl/maps/U8s6VwjqC4K2

Phone :+358 9 43427640
Address:Runeberginkatu 55b, 00260 Helsinki

47

Exploring The Legendary Landmarks in Helsinki

There's this unique church in Helsinki. Its underground interior is composed of Helsinki peninsula's solid rock.

Tuomo Suomalainen and Timo Suomalainen designed it in the 1960s. It shows a shallow circular dome of glass borne and copper sheeting on concrete ribs. Its inside features a glazed dome where exquisite natural light permeates.

It attracted a string of controversies from religious sectors. A few of its nicknames before include "devil defense bunker" and "million mark church". Despite the negative side to its reputation, its popularity for musicians remains. Mainly because of its amazing acoustics, the church is used as a venue for musical events.

It's called *Helsinki's Rock Church or Temppeliaukio*. It's one of the plethora of legendary attractions in the city.

Helsinki's Rock Church Website
http://www.helsinginkirkot.fi/en/churches/
rock-church-temppeliaukio
Helsinki's Rock ChurchMap

https://goo.gl/maps/yMgsKjdF4yo

Phone :+358 9 23406320

Address:Lutherinkatu 3, 00100 Helsinki

What Makes an Attraction Legendary?

There are countless landmarks all around Helsinki. While they're all important, some landmarks are a notch more fascinating. Others prefer to hop on a plane and travel hundreds, if not thousands, of miles just to catch a glimpse.

When you're in Helsinki, maybe you should join a flock of travelers who visit a particular landmark.

Top five attractions:

(1)Kauppatori (or Market Square and Salutorget)

Kauppatori, on the harbor side, is a tourist favorite in Helsinki. Especially during spring and autumn, it's loaded with activities. You can check out different stalls as you walk around.

Most travelers usually hang out in the area. They stroll with snacks in hand. You can follow their lead, too. But, try not to be caught off guard if a seagull grabs your snack. The animal is with many others of its kind.

What to expect:
- Outdoor cafes
- Fresh fish (for sale)
- Scarves (mostly during the winter season)
- Knit hats (mostly during the winter season)
- Furs (mostly during the winter season)
- Organic products (for sale)
- Ferry cruise service
- Finnish foods (for sale)
- Finnish souvenirs (for sale)
- Exhibition of old American cars

Kauppatori Map
https://goo.gl/maps/JEsAvzYfDHQ2
Phone :+358 9 31023565
Address:Eteläranta, 00170 Helsinki

(2)The Fortress of Suomenlinna (& the island of Suomenlinna)

In the 1700s, Sweden built a fortress in the island of Suomenlinna for Russia's protection. This building is called The Fortress of Suomenlinna.

In the old days, there was nothing much to see, but a fortress. Today, the place has gone up another level. The fortress' restoration made it a thing of beauty. It became a magnificent site, and the people behind UNESCO agree. It's been named a World Heritage Site.

To visit The Fortress of Suomenlinna, purchasing a ticket for a roundtrip ferry ride is a good idea. For no more than €4, the destination is yours to explore.

What to expect:
· Finnish Castle

- Canons
- Cafes
- Residential buildings
- Restaurants
- Theaters

The Fortress of Suomenlinna Website
http://www.suomenlinna.fi/en/
The Fortress of Suomenlinna Map
https://goo.gl/maps/DAuN4dJzh1s
Phone :+358 29 5338410

(3)The Helsinki Cathedral

Especially if you're a fan of neoclassical architecture, don't miss The Helsinki Cathedral. It was built as a tribute to Finland's Grand Duke, Tsar Nicholas the first of Russia. Its completion took twenty-two years (from 1830 to 1852).

Other times, The Helsinki Cathedral is called The Lutheran Cathedral. It resembles a Greek cross with four pieces of equilateral arms. It's a distinctive landmark in Helsinki because of its tall dome that is surrounded by smaller domes.

What to expect:
- Statue of Emperor Alexander the second (at the front façade)
- Life-size statues of Twelve Apostles (at the apex and corners)
- Russian-donated altarpiece
- Free-standing bell towers
- Cylindrical pulpit

The Helsinki Cathedral Website
http://www.helsinginkirkot.fi/en/churches/cathedral
The Helsinki Cathedral Map
https://goo.gl/maps/s3Z9aYwc1RH2
Phone :+358 9 23406120
Address:Unioninkatu 29, 00170 Helsinki

(4)Korkeasaari Elaintarha (or Helsinki Zoo)

Korkeasaari Elaintarha is the ideal place for an animal lover. It has been around since 1889! Its location is on a 22-hectare rocky island that connects the mainland with a bridge. It's Helsinki's biggest zoo and one of Finland's most popular attractions.

It's also called the Helsinki Zoo. An observation tower is available so you can check out the animals from a high point. It's open to the public all year round. You can get there via a ferry, a private car, or a bus.

<u>What to expect (animals):</u>
- Amur leopard
- Barbary macaques
- Eurasian brown bear
- European otters
- Guanaco
- Hamadyras baboons
- Siberian tiger
- Takin
- Turkmenian kulan
- Wild horse

Korkeasaari Elaintarha Website
http://www.korkeasaari.fi/helsinki-zoo/
Korkeasaari Elaintarha Map
https://goo.gl/maps/MhmSKtYBD272
<u>Phone :</u>+358 9 3101615
<u>Address:</u>Mustikkamaanpolku 12, 00270 Helsinki

(5)The Sibelius Monument & Park

Are you interested in stopping by at a place that features an outstanding result of a fundraising campaign?

If so, The Sibelius Monument & Park is for you!

The centerpiece of the park is the Sibelius Monument or Passio Musicae. It came to be because of a debate about abstract art – its flaws and merits. It's a sculpture created by Eila Hiltunen. It's intended to honor the famous musical composer, Jean Sibelius.

What to expect:
- The Sibelius Monument (made of welded pipes that resemble organ pipes)
- A relaxing environment

The Sibelius Monument & Park Website
http://www.eilahiltunen.net/monument.html
The Sibelius Monument & Park Map
https://goo.gl/maps/VNmEdFYRmmq
<u>Phone :</u>+358 9 31087041
<u>Address:</u>Sibeliuksen puisto, Mechelininkatu, 00250 Helsinki

48

It's Museum Time: Best Museums in Helsinki

An exhibition of a taxidermist's prized possessions is among the things that a museum in Helsinki has in store for you.

For one, would you be excited to see an African elephant (that a taxidermist worked on) at a museum lobby?

With an up close encounter, among the things that you can observe about an African elephant are:
- It has a thick body
- It has large ears
- Its nose and upper lip create a trunk
- It has four molars
- It has stocky legs
- It has a concave back

If you don't mind spotting a taxidermed elephant at a museum, you're probably set on discovering more about other animals. A perfect place for you is a museum!

A Great Reason to Visit a Museum

A trip to a museum is usually worthwhile. You can learn important information, and see exclusive items. Overall, after your trip, you end up happier.

Museums feature a variety of things. Seeing these things makes you feel good. Whether you're on your trip alone or with a group, a museum is a good place to visit.

In Helsinki, there are many brilliant museums for you to check out!

Top five museums:

(1)The Bank of Finland Museum

To find out more about the monetary economics, Helsinki's The Bank of Finland Museum has got you covered. You can see exhibitions about the operations of the bank, as well as the operations of those with an instrumental part in the Finnish society.

If you think financial matters are cryptic, esoteric, and dull, a trip to The Bank of Finland Museum will make you re-think. Because the presentations come with a fun factor, you just might walk out with loads of new knowledge and a smile!

Phone :+358 10 8312981
Address: 2 Snellmaninkatu

On display
· History of money
· Banknote art
· Bonds
· Writings about International Monetary Integration
· Monetary policy

- Mutual debt concepts
- Highlights from the Helsinki Stock Exchange
- The Bank of Finland's statistics

The Bank of Finland
http://www.rahamuseo.fi/en/
The Bank of Finland Museum Map
https://goo.gl/maps/NWvyvgBjWd22

(2)The National Museum of Finland

The National Museum of Finland will show you the history of Finland from the stone age until today.The museum is located in central Helsinki.

Phone :+358 29 5336000
Address :34 Mannerheimintie

On display:
· History of Finland

The National Museum of Finland Website
http://www.kansallismuseo.fi/en/nationalmuseum
The National Museum of Finland Map
https://goo.gl/maps/YwuL7NdAp262

(3)Sederholm House

To spend time in a historical playground, the Sederholm House is the place to be! It's in a central location so finding it is almost effortless.

Since it was built back in 1757, it's a lot like your grandparents' house. A visit can trigger memories of visiting a traditional house. The building is Helsinki's oldest one, as you can observe from the interiors.

Phone :+358 9 31036630
Address:18 Aleksanterinkatu

On display
- 18th century boutique
- 18th century playground
- Puppets
- Early century clothing

Sederholm House Website
http://www.helsinginkaupunginmuseo.fi/en/
julkaisut/sederholm-house/
Sederholm House Map
https://goo.gl/maps/iS8ZqifrSkA2

(4)Helsinki Civil Defense Museum

The Helsinki Civil Defense Museum privileges you with a peek at arrangements regarding the city's civil defense. There, you can view the history and present-day strategies for the promotion of security during wars.

A visit to the museum is one-of-a-kind. It's not limited to viewing items. It includes a thrilling experience with dramatic sound effects of collapsing buildings and dropping bombs.

Phone :+358 9 278 2285
Address: 16B Siltaveuorenranta

On display
- Gears for crisis situations
- Gears for protection against gas poisoning and radiation
- Bomb shelter; an exhibition of preparations during the Continuation War in the 1940s

· Safety equipment

Helsinki Civil Defense Museum Website
http://hvssy.fi/museoeng/
Helsinki Civil Defense Museum Map
https://goo.gl/maps/93Y5c7h74j32

(5)Natural History Museum

At the introduction of this chapter, a feature of the Natural History Museum is shared. Apart from an African elephant on display at the lobby, there are different collections (with up to 13, 000, 000 pieces) inside. With all the items on display, the aim is to promote environmental awareness.

Since its erection in 1913, the building continues to receive praises for its flamboyant architecture – unusually flamboyant architecture. It displays a laidback concept with a touch of Gothic style. The Russian architects, M.G. Chayko and Lev P. Chicko, deserve thanks.

Phone :+358 29 4128800
Address: 13 Pohjoinen Rautatiekatu

On display
· Animal collection
· Fossil samples
· Geological collection
· Plant collection
· Mycological collection
· Mineral collection

Natural History Museum Website
https://www.facebook.com/
luonnontieteellinenmuseo
Natural History Museum Map
https://goo.gl/maps/gLnatfhftmT2

49

Appreciation for the Arts: Top 5 Art Galleries

When you're in Helsinki, a must-see is the *Ateneum*.

The Ateneum is an art museum with direct affiliations to the Finnish National Gallery. Theodore Hoijer completed it in 1887.

Previously, it's the home of Helsinki University of Art and Design and Finland's Academy of Fine Arts.

Its location is on the Helsinki center – near the Helsinki Central Railway Station. When it comes to classical art, it has by far the biggest collection.

Some of the classical artworks inside are *The Aino Myth* (by Akseli Gallen-Kallela) and *The Wounded Angel* (by Hugo Simberg).

Phone :+358 29 4500401
Address:Kaivokatu 2, 00100 Helsinki

Ateneum Website
http://www.ateneum.fi/thats-how-it-used-to-be-or
-was-it-thematic-tour/?lang=en
Ateneum Map
https://goo.gl/maps/nvyMu3YVJAn

What Makes Art Galleries Magical?

Art galleries are magical places. They boost your creativity, enrich your mind, and improve your emotional strength. With the loads of different art collections, your creative side gets a treat.

Because Helsinki has a handful of art galleries, your trip is going to be more worthwhile if you show up at one!

Top five art galleries:

(1)Forum Box

Forum Box, an artist-managed gallery, is a cooperative that aims to enrich the cultural life in Helsinki. It stands in a space that's formerly a cold storage room. Since its initial opening in 1999, visitors would flock to the place to check out modern art works.

Artists:

- Adel Abidin
- Emilia Ukkonon

Phone :+358 9 68550080
Address:Ruoholahdenranta 3A, 00180 Helsinki
Forum Box Website
http://www.forumbox.fi/en/home/
Forum Box Map
https://goo.gl/maps/F4Z5JPnzSrK2

(2)Galleria Ama

Situated in a very flexible space is Galleria Ama. It welcomes all sorts of artworks from Finnish artists. Its focus is on present-day artworks of many forms. The exhibits include paintings, sculptures, installation, and photography.

Artists
- Kaisaleena Halinen
- Thomas Nyqvist

Phone :+358 50 589 4969
Address:Rikhardinkatu 1, 00130 Helsinki

Galleria Ama Website

http://ama.fi/
Galleria Ama Map
https://goo.gl/maps/ywYFp91UQK52

(3)Kuntshalle

Kuntshalle is an exhibition venue for modern art, architecture, and design. Its owner is a private foundation that receives support from the city. The place is a masterpiece of its own by highlighting an exquisite sample of Nordic Classicism.

Artists:

- Niki de St. Phalle
- Eero Aarnio
- Marlene Dumas
- Andy Warhol
- Helmut Newton
- Karin Mamma Andersson

Kuntshalle Website
http://taidehalli.fi/en/taidehalli/#p39
Kuntshalle Map
https://goo.gl/maps/UHMkicTiykF2

Phone :+358 9 4542060
Address:Nervanderinkatu 3, 00100 Helsinki

(4)Galerie Anhava

Galerie Anhava is among Helsinki's foremost modern art galleries. Since its establishment in 1991, it went on to become a top-notch gallery for the international art scene. It features paintings, sculp-

tures, photography, and video artworks.
Artists:
- Antti Laitinen
- Jorma Hautala

Phone : +358 9 669 989
Address:Fredrikinkatu, 00120

Galerie Anhava Website
http://www.anhava.com/
Galerie Anhava Map
https://goo.gl/maps/EdjFw7myJY52

(5)Sinne

Sinne is an art gallery and organization that promotes the visual art scene in Helsinki's Swedish-speaking portions. With its primary goal of nurturing future artistic talents, it features experimental sculptures, installations, and different art pieces. Because of its theme, it's an ideal hangout for the young artist who shows some potential.

Address: 16 Iso Roobertinkatu
Artists:
- Jaakko Pallasvuo
- Kimmo Modig
- Sari Palosaari

Sinne Website

http://sinne.proartibus.fi/en/frontpage/
Sinne Map
https://goo.gl/maps/8K9CtYd8KRL2

Phone:+358 45 8833716
Address:Iso Roobertinkatu 16, 00120 Helsinki

50

The Best-Tasting Coffee: Top 5 Coffee Shops

Helsinki is known for its dreamy coffee scene. First, the scene revolved around the sizes of coffee mugs and cinnamon rolls. Then, the craze proceeded to lattes, espressos, and espresso-based coffee.

Nowadays, as most baristas in Helsinki agree, the coffee scene is about quality coffee + relaxing setting. It's no longer about the kinds of coffee, the sizes of the coffee mugs, or the additions to the drink. Today, it's more on the flavor of the coffee.

Why Go to a Coffee Shop?

A reason to go to a coffee shop is to receive a boost of enthusiasm. Downing the drink would make you feel more energetic and be more alert before exploring the city's wonders. Whether it's in the morning or afternoon (or even at night), you can always have a cup.

In Helsinki, the best coffee shops are just around the corner!

Top 5 coffee shops:

Café Regatta

Café Regatta is situated in a small fishing village. Inside, it displays pans, pots, shoes, and other vintage items. It serves cinnamon buns and affordable coffee with free refills.

Phone:+358 40 0760049
Address:10 Merikannontie
Café Regatta Website
https://www.facebook.com/Cafe-Regatta-official-125305227553336/
Café Regatta Map
https://goo.gl/maps/nLvAd1rgYrp

Johan and Nystrom

Johan and Nystrom is a tall coffee shop. It features tall ceilings, bulky walls, and bright-colored cushions. Though the place can seem overwhelming, the atmosphere is cozy. Inside, you can revel at a slice (or more of cheesecake, great-tasting coffee, and chocolate.

Phone:+358 40 5203623
Address: 7 Kanavaranta
Johan and Nystrom Website
http://johanochnystrom.se/en/about-us/our-places/helsinki/
Johan and Nystrom Map
https://goo.gl/maps/wiZ6rcpjceS2

Good Life Coffee

If you ask locals where the best coffee is served, Good Life Coffee is most likely the answer that comes up. They roast their own coffee. Their specialty? Filter coffee!

Phone:+358 50 3808961
Address: 17 Kolmas Linja
Good Life Coffee Website
http://goodlifecoffee.fi/
Good Life Coffee Map
https://goo.gl/maps/AS9LvuvDxR52

La Torrefazione

With an ideal location on a shopping street, La Torrefazzione is awesome when it comes to a quick cup of coffee. Alongside coffee, it delights guests with hot chocolate, goat cheese, red pesto, and other delicious sandwiches.

Phone:+358 9 42890648
Address: 50 B Aleksanderinkatu
La Torrefazione Website

http://www.latorre.fi/en/
La Torrefazione Map
https://goo.gl/maps/myuULyK3gum

Moko

Moko is a store and coffee shop combination.Moko makes the list because the location is great, and the interior is beautiful.The coffee isn't the best in town, but the atmosphere in Moko makes it well worth the visit.

Phone:+358 10 3156156
Address: Perämiehenkatu 10
Moko Website
http://moko.fi/in-english/
Moko Map
https://goo.gl/maps/bskLDzoJwFH2

51

How to Enjoy a Night in Helsinki: Top 5 Night Clubs

Spending a night out in Helsinki?

Make your night count by going to a night club! Because the locals are their own version of accommodating, it's not rare for you to meet a friend.

With beer, food, and great music, you can be as merry as desired with your new mate.

Let him share a story of his life.

Let him tell you about a friend.

Let him talk about his sentiments with you.

Let him narrate his day.

And perhaps, let him give you travel advice.

Let him be for an hour or more and you're unlikely to regret it in the morning. All the fun is possible if you visit one of the night clubs in the city!

Why Check in at a Night Club?

Like in most places, Helsinki's nightlife is fascinating. A reason to check in at one of the city's night clubs is that it's a source of pure fun at night. When most of the locals are asleep, others are too energetic not to have a splendid time.

If you want to experience the city's vibrant nightlife and be jolly until you pass out, a night club's a great place to be!

Top 5 nightclubs:

(1)Ateljee Baari

Ateljee Baari has a very edgy atmosphere that attracts the classy locals. It's a famous night club. Apart from the foods and drinks, people visit to catch a breathtaking view of the rooftops in Helsinki.

Phone:+358 9 43366340
Address:5 Kalevankatu
Ateljee Baari Website
https://www.raflaamo.fi/en/helsinki/atelje-bar
Ateljee Baari Map
https://goo.gl/maps/ay7pTiv7oTA2

(2)Nightclub Kaarle XII

A night club that houses six bars in the venue is Nightclub Karle XII. It has a nice setting that is complemented by dancing pop music. The usual crowd inside is composed of the young and the restless.

Phone:+358 20 7701470
Address:40 Kasarmikatu
Nightclub Kaarle XII Website
https://www.facebook.com/KaarleXII/
Nightclub Kaarle XII Map
https://goo.gl/maps/zFVYEwiniUr

(3)The Tavastia and Semifinal Nightclubs

The Tavastia and Semifinal Nightclubs are originally two night clubs. They've been merged to attract more audiences from Helsinki. It features wonderful live music from folks in Europe and the US.

Phone:+358 9 77467420
Address: 4 to Kekkosenkatu
The Tavastia and Semifinal Nightclubs Website

http://www.tavastiaklubi.fi/en_GB/
The Tavastia and Semifinal Nightclubs Map
https://goo.gl/maps/1mwfqZLVuP32

(4)Le Bonk

Le Bonk is a stylish club with a fantastic atmosphere.The focus of this club is not rock music; it's more of a glitz and glamor type of club.So if you are looking for something different, then this club is for you.This club has a nice terrace and is a great place to dance the night away.Sometimes Le Bonk has live music.

Phone:+358 40 5646661
Address:Yrjönkatu 24
Le Bonk Website
https://www.facebook.com/lebonkhelsinki
Le Bonk Map
https://goo.gl/maps/xFxJjG4ZdXH2

(5)Kuudes Linja

If you want to enjoy a wild night of partying and dancing with a live DJ, then go to Kuudes Linja.They play a variety of music ranging from reggae to techno.

Phone:+358 40 5397599
Address:Hämeentie 13 B
Kuudes Linja Website
https://www.facebook.com/kuudeslinja
Kuudes Linja Map
https://goo.gl/maps/mq9NGTEGUB12

52

Only in Helsinki: The Special Things that You Can Do in the City

The Töölönlahti Bay is one of Helsinki's gems. You can access it by first, heading to the city center, then walking along a circular path. Surrounding it is a number of famous establishments such as *The Parliament House, Sininen Villa, and Finlandia House.*

It's set in a relaxing environment, and it boasts of a majestic view. While it's usually a quiet retreat, joggers can sometimes crowd the bay.

A majestic site in the bay is *The Winter Gardens*. You can find it at the northern area. Since it features a plethora of plants, the place is a treat for plant-lovers.

The*Töölönlahti Bay* is just one Helsinki attraction. When walking around the city, there's more for you to explore.

Töölönlahti Bay Map
https://goo.gl/maps/nDcg9U5WXA42

Your Very Own City Tour

Don't forget that Helsinki is a hodgepodge of architecture. The establishments feature beautiful designs including *Jugend or Art Nouveau, Neoclassical, Vernacular, and Modern-Day architecture.*

Checking out the different buildings all around the city is a treat. It's as if you are learning about its personality and its history.

Thus, feel free to plan a personal city tour. Walk around, take the bus, go on board a tram, or ride a car. You don't have to do anything per se. You simply have to admire your surroundings.

Helsinki Bus Tour Website
http://www.redbuses.com/hop-on-hop-off-helsinki/

Linnanmäki Amusement Park: A Fun-Filled Destination

Hungry for a psychedelic experience in Finland's tallest roller coaster?

If so, prepare to be blown away by the *Vonkaptuous* at Linnanmäki Amusement Park.

The Vonkaptuous is just one thrilling ride at the amusement. There are more than thirty amusement rides within the place. Among the choices are bumper cars, water and steel roller coasters, carousels, octopus rides, Ferris wheels, and galloping horse rides.

Phone:+358 10 5722200
Address:Tivolikuja 1, 00510 Helsinki
Linnanmäki Amusement Park Website
http://www.linnanmaki.fi/en
Linnanmäki Amusement Park Map
https://goo.gl/maps/s8nebfwFFJF2

Relax at Central Park

Keskuspuisto or Helsinki's central park is the place to be for a relaxing time. It's an incredibly massive park at the heart of the city. It features a manicured garden, walking trails, biking paths, and an entrance to a forest.

In the park, you can sit down for a picnic, enjoy mindless laughter with new friends or just chill. Especially if you want to take a break and view the life in Helsinki, finding a spot at central park is a great idea.

Phone:+358 9 3101673
Central Park Website
http://www.hel.fi/hel2/keskuspuisto/
eng/1centralpark/
Central Park Map
https://goo.gl/maps/xXxptc3ygbx

Visit the Olympic Stadium

Helsinki's Olympic Stadium is a one-of-a-kind place. It's located at the top of a lake and to the northern area of a large hall. It's a famous venue of historical matches, and it houses a 72m tower and a museum.

To feel majestic and appreciate an amazing view of Helsinki, take a trip to the stadium.

Phone:+358 9 4366010
Address:Paavo Nurmen tie 1, 00250 Helsinki
Olympic Stadium Map
https://goo.gl/maps/WBsRJMseCk72

53

Mind Your Safety

Did you know that Helsinki is crowned as the most honest city in the world?

According to a study conducted by the team at the Readers' Digest, eleven out of twelve locals would willingly return a wallet that's not their own. Compared to locals in Mumbai (India) and Lisbon

(Portugal), it's an outstanding record.

With honest locals, Helsinki seems to be a safe zone for you. Isn't it comforting to be surrounded by trustworthy folks who have their hearts on the right place?

Why Mind Your Safety?

Minding your safety while travelling brings you peace of mind. It's important to know what to expect beforehand. Doing so allows you to prepare. Because you feel secure, you become less anxious of the possibilities. Ultimately, you can enjoy your trip even more.

It's a good thing that Helsinki is reputed as one of the safest places in the world. It wouldn't hurt to keep in mind a few safety tips.

Safety tips:

Watch Out!
- Watch out for drunkards. The locals in Helsinki are quite merry and joyful. It's a good thing. But, when they've had too much to drink, they can be too much. Fortunately, an exhibition of violent behavior is rare. Stay away from them, though. They can drive you nuts!
- The sight of panhandlers and beggars isn't rare. Since they can be very persistent, you may want to avoid these people on the streets.
- A snowy day in June? In Helsinki, it isn't rare. Be ready with clothes for protection against a spontaneous cold weather.
- Borreolosis is a disease caused by mites. When hanging out at sea sides, be watchful of small animals. Mites might infest these animals.

Road Safety

- Be careful of slippery roads and tram stops. Helsinki accommodates snow many days of the year. When snow melts, some places can be unsafe for mindless walking.
- Always keep your eyes on the road when driving. It's not rare for moose and white-tailed deer to cross the streets.

Roaming around

- Always pay attention to the walk signs when crossing the streets. Since they can change swiftly, they pose threats for slow pedestrians.
- When walking around the city, please stick to pedestrian crossing lanes. Some drivers have the tendency to drive extraordinarily fast.

Helsinki Emergency Numbers

General emergencies call- 112
Helsinki Emergency Website
http://www.hel.fi/www/Helsinki/en/
socia-health/health/emergency

54

Experiencing Helsinki: A 3-Day Travel Itinerary

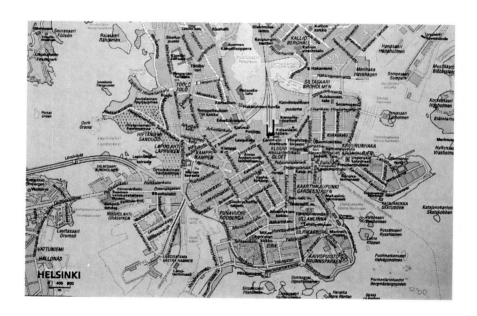

If you plan to visit Helsinki for three days, make sure to maximize your trip. After choosing a quality hotel, stop by at the finest places in Helsinki. The city in Finland is an awesome city to travel to. Let your stay be a memorable one!

A tip is to create an itinerary. Set a schedule, organize, and make priorities. Based on the information throughout this book, you have a good idea of the wonders of Helsinki.

Here's a sample 3-day itinerary. You can use it as it is, or use it and modify some parts according to preference.

Day 01
TIME
· **ACTIVITY**
· **VENUE**

7:00 AM to 8:00 AM
   · Have coffee and breakfast
   · Good Life Coffee

8:00 AM to 9:00 AM
   · Walk around the city
   · Helsinki

9:00 AM to 10:00 AM
   · Visit a museum
   · Natural History Museum

10 AM to 12:00 noon
   · Have lunch
   · Juuri

12:00 noon to 1:00 PM
   · Check out a legendary attraction
   · The Helsinki Cathedral

1:00 PM to 2:00 PM

- Go to an art gallery
- Gallerie Anhava

2:00 PM To 3:00 PM
- Have coffee and some snacks
- Johann and Nystrom

3:00 PM to 4:00 PM
- Visit a museum
- Helsinki Civil Defense Museum

4:00 PM to 5:00 PM
- Hang out a relaxing place
- Central Park

5:00 PM to 7:00 PM
- Have dinner
- Chef & Somelier

7:00 PM TO 8:00 PM
- Go to an art gallery
- Sinne

9:00 PM to 10:00 PM
- Have a drink at a bar
- Liberty or death

Day 02
<u>TIME</u>
- **<u>ACTIVITY</u>**
- **VENUE**

<u>7:00 AM to 8:00 AM</u>
- Have coffee and breakfast
- Moko Café

<u>8:00 AM to 10:00 AM</u>
- Check out a legendary attraction
- Korkeasaari Elaintarha

<u>10 AM to 12:00 noon</u>
- Have lunch
- Ragu

<u>12:00 noon to 1:00 PM</u>
- Visit a museum
- Sederholm House

<u>1:00 PM to 2:00 PM</u>
- Go to an art gallery
- Forum Box

<u>2:00 PM To 3:00 PM</u>
- Roam around the city
- Helsinki

<u>3:00 PM to 4:00 PM</u>
- Visit a museum
- The National Museum of Finland

4:00 PM to 5:00 PM
- Check out a legendary attraction
- The Sibelius Monument & Park

5:00 PM to 7:00 PM
- Have dinner
- Ravintola Tokyo55

8:00 PM to 9:00 PM
- Have a drink at a bar
- Siltannen

9:00 PM to 10:00 PM
- Have a drink at another bar
- Bar Bäkkäri

10:00 PM to 11:00 PM
- Go to a night club
- Nightclub Kaarle XII

Day 03
TIME
- **ACTIVITY**
- **VENUE**

7:00 AM to 8:00 AM
- Have coffee and breakfast
- Café Regatta

8:00 AM to 9:00 AM
- Go somewhere majestic
- Olympic Stadium

9:00 AM to 10:00 AM
- Visit a museum
- The Bank of Finland Museum

10 AM to 12:00 noon
- Have lunch and buy souvenirs
- Kauppatori

12:00 noon to 1:00 PM
- Go somewhere majestic
- Linnanmäki Amusement Park

1:00 PM to 2:00 PM
- Go to an art gallery
- Kuntshalle

2:00 PM To 3:00 PM
- Have coffee and some snacks
- La Torrefazione

3:00 PM to 5:00 PM
- Hang out a relaxing place
- The Fortress of Suomenlinna

5:00 PM to 7:00 PM
- Have dinner
- Nokka

7:00 PM TO 8:00 PM
- Go to an art gallery
- Galleria Ama

8:00 PM to 9:00 PM
- Have a drink at a bar
- Bar Molotow

9:00 PM to 10:00 PM
- Have a drink at another bar
- Musta Kissa

10:00 PM to 11:00 PM
- Go to a night club
- Kuudes Linja

55

OSLO INTRODUCTION

Most people know that Oslo is the Scandinavian country of Norway's capital city. However, not all people know that Oslo has plenty of attractions to offer the adventurous local and international traveler.

Surrounded by hills, forests, and lakes, Oslo can be considered an undiscovered gem. Oslo is not as well-traveled as metropolitan areas like Paris, New York, or London, or even fellow Scandinavian cities like Stockholm or Copenhagen. Nevertheless, travelers to Norway – at some point – will pass through Oslo. And those who have done so will leave the city pleasantly surprised.

You won't be coming to Oslo to soak under the sun. Instead, you'll be coming here for winter- or nature-related activities. The city is also close to nature as its parks and countryside offer opportunities for cycling, hiking, boating, and skiing.

Like any other city in the world, Oslo allows you to indulge in activities like dining at restaurants, seeing city landmarks, and visiting museums and art galleries. Oslo's architectural landmarks are also extraordinary.

When you're not touring the city and its outskirts, you can relax at any of its coffee shops, bars, and nightclubs. There are also other activities that you can experience only in this bustling Norwegian city.

Oslo is indeed an easy-going metropolis with an atmosphere that is friendly to families. It's also a progressive city with a vibrant gay scene. Cultural activities and the nightlife scene are diverse. In short, Oslo offers a wide range of attractions to match your personal interests and tastes.

56

Brief History and Background

Oslo's documented history dates back to around 1000 CE. Since the Medieval times, Oslo has undergone multiple changes, including several name changes, too.

Oslo, which is the city's current name, was also the city's first name. During the Medieval times, the settlement was located east of the Bjørvika inlet. King Christian IV, after a fire in 1624, had the town rebuilt in an area underneath the Akershus Fortress. He then renamed Oslo to Christiania. It then reverted to the present name – Oslo – in 1925.

Oslo in the Middle Ages

The first town-like settlement may have been built around 1000 CE. Medieval Oslo was located between the Ekeberg hills, on the Bjørvika inlet's east side. Around 1300 CE, the town had about 3,000 inhabitants. King Haakon V, who reigned from 1299 to 1319, had commissioned the construction of the Akershus Fortress.

In the Old Town (Gamlebyen), you'll see medieval Oslo's cultural layers, building parts, and ruins. The old town is also the location of Oslo Ladegård's Medieval Office, which is an information office that sets up guided tours of the old town. Nearby is the memorial park with ruins of the St. Olav convent and the 12th century St. Hallvard cathedral.

Renaissance Oslo

In 1536, Norway united with Denmark. After the 1624 fire, King Christian IV of Denmark ordered the new settlement to be built below the Akershus Fortress. You can also find several well-preserved 17th-century buildings in Oslo. In Kvadraturen, you can see Oslo's old town hall as well as Café Engebret, which is the city's oldest restaurant.

The New Capital

In 1814, Denmark ceded Norway to King Karl Johan of Sweden. Norway then had its own constitution. On May 17, 1814, Christiania (renamed Oslo in 1925) became Norway's capital. In 1825, King Karl

Johan started building the Royal Palace, which was completed in 1848 during King Oscar I's reign. The Parliament (Storting) building in Karl Johans gate was completed in 1866.

The industrial age in Norway started in 1850. Between 1850 and 1900, Christiania's population surged from around 30,000 to 230,000, due to an influx of rural-based workers.

A City Steeped in History

Oslo has undergone major changes because of redevelopment and fires, and most of the original town is gone. In certain neighborhoods, however, you can still get a sense of the past.

The Akershus Fortress for example, which has stood for over 700 years, is a vital cultural landmark. Many Norwegian patriots during World War II were executed here, and the fortress was ceded to the

Norwegian resistance movement in the war's final moments. Vidkun Quisling, after the war, was imprisoned in the fortress. Norway's Resistance Museum is also located within the fortress grounds.

Frogner Park is where you'll find the Oslo City Museum. The museum presents photos, objects, and models that put together a comprehensive picture of cultural and commercial activities, city development, and street life through the city's lengthy history.

The Akerselva River was Norway's cradle of industrialization. Walking along the river can be a pleasant experience, with old wooden houses and water cascades contrasting with massive industrial buildings.

57

Best Time to Go and Weather

The best time to go to Oslo is from May to September. During such time, the temperature averages around 15°C and there about 10 days of rain during September.

The late spring to summer to early autumn months may be the time when you can experience milder temperatures. It may get chilly, though, so it's important to bring along a coat. Despite the temperature changes, Oslo offers the adventurer year-round activities. Let's see what every season has to offer for the Oslo visitor.

Oslo Temperatures

Winter (November to March)
Average Temperature: 0.7°C to 4.3°C
Lowest Temperature: −15.3°C
Maximum Temperature: 13.2°C

Spring (April to May)
Average Temperature: 4.5 to 10.8°C
Lowest Temperature: 2.4°C
Maximum Temperature: 25.2°C

Summer (June to August)
Average Temperature: 15.2°C to 16.4°C
Lowest Temperature: 6.1°C
Maximum Temperature: 30.5°C

Autumn (September to October)
Average Temperature: 6.3°C to 10.8°C
Lowest Temperature: 0.2°C
Maximum Temperature: 22.5°C

Set on the same latitude as most of Siberia and Alaska, Norway (including Oslo) has four distinct seasons, with each season having its character and benefits of visiting. Due to the Gulf Stream's warm air currents, temperatures tend to be more pleasant in the country's south than in the country's north.

Winter

In November, which is the start of the Norwegian winter, temperatures can drop considerably. The season is characterized by bitter cold and the lack of daylight. While snow can cover most of northern Norway, snow rarely settles along the southern coastal cities and towns – including Oslo.

At this point, Oslo can be an excellent starting off point if you want to go to areas having winter attractions. Norway then becomes a winter wonderland with excellent dog-sledging, skiing, snowmobiling, and ice fishing opportunities. In Oslo, you can still enjoy snow sports as there's a ski resort within the city's limits.

While it's cheaper to go to Norway during the winter, services are reduced. Thus, you need to plan for contingencies and plan your trip well if you seek to visit the country during this time. Precipitation comes down as snow from December to February.

Spring

As temperatures become warmer, the flowers start to bloom; the snow melts, and daytime become longer. Spring is graced with light showers, and the snow starts to melt during March. Spring is a wonderful time to visit the green landscapes, flowering orchards, and swollen waterfalls.

During April, there can be nightly subzero temperatures, which can cause melted snow to refreeze – leading to potentially dangerous road conditions. While early spring can be chilly, late spring can reach temperatures of 14°C.

Summer

When the sun is out during summers in Oslo, temperatures in the low 20s can be enjoyed immensely. The warmest months are August and July with temperatures in the low 20s. The temperatures rarely rise up to the 30s, and the nightly temperature usually dips to the teens.

During summers, you can do pretty much anything, except ski. You can hike through the woods, head out into the city, see the old city of Oslo, enjoy shopping, attend an outdoor concert, or indulge in the vibrant nightclub scene.

The winds blowing in from the Atlantic can make the summers unpredictable. You may end up visiting a sunny Oslo or a wet one with frequent rains. Rainfall increases during the start of summer and peaks in August.

The amount of daylight is one of the best things about the Norwegian summer. In June, there are around 5 hours between sunset and sunrise. While swimming in 17°C waters (even during summer) is not pleasant for most people, there are others who seek the cold and just jump right in.

Autumn

The season is wet and cold, and temperatures drop quickly. Days are becoming short. Autumn temperatures drop from 14°C in September to 7°C in October. Frost develops at night at the beginning of October, and there's a lot of rainfall during the season. It may get too cold, and rain can turn to snow. The average temperature at the end of autumn is about −1°C.

Autumn is also a good time to enjoy outdoor activities, as the countryside and forests turn into vibrant shades of orange and red. Wild fruit is ripest at September and crab is at its prime. Autumn is best for photography aficionados who want to capture the change in seasons. Foodies can also find autumns in Oslo appealing.

58

Transportation

Oslo's city center is small and can be navigated on foot. The suburbs, however, fan out to great distances, which warrants a metro-wide integrated public transportation system that consists of metro, trains, and buses to help you navigate the city and the surrounding counties.

Oslo Map
https://goo.gl/maps/LehMya4mqER2

Ruter AS coordinates public transport in Oslo and the nearby Akershus County, and individual operators are contracted to run specific services. Ruter controls pricing, planning, and managing the entire transport system. Ruter's tickets are valid for trams, buses, subways, local trains, and ferries (excluding the Bygdøy ferry).

Transfers to and From Gardermoen International Airport

The FlyToget train is the fastest way to and from the Oslo Airport in Gardermoen. In 19 minutes, FlyToget's shuttles connect the airport to the central station in Oslo.

Gardermoen International Airport Website
https://avinor.no/en/airport/oslo-airport/
Gardermoen International Airport Map
https://goo.gl/maps/7DawRRjUJcM2
Phone:+47 64 81 20 00

FlyToget Train Website

http://www.flytoget.no/flytoget_eng

Phone:+47 23 15 90 00

e-mail:flytoget@flytoget.no

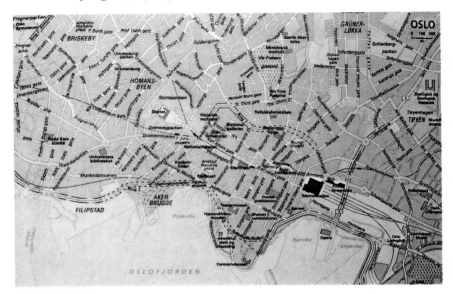

Between 4:40 am and midnight, trains depart every 10-20 minutes. Certain trains end at the central station, while others travel further to the National Theatre and stop south, ending at Drammen.

If you're traveling on a budget, you can ride the standard NSB (Norwegian State Railways) intercity and local train services that stop at Gardermoen (NOK90 for 26 minutes). One Norwegian Krone (NOK) is approximately $0.12 or (€)0.11. From the city, you can ride the trains at certain central stations including Oslo S. and Nationalteatret. The price is half that of FlyToget, and nearly as fast. However, NSB doesn't run as frequently as FlyToget.

Norwegian State Railways Website(NSB)
https://www.nsb.no/en/frontpage
Phone: 815 00 888 / (+47) 61 05 19 10

The equivalent of NSB, Flybussen, departs from the Gardermoen airport and ends at the Galleri Oslo terminal. It also serves few other city stops every 20 minutes from 4:00 am to about 10:00 pm. The trip from the airport, which takes about 40 minutes, costs NOK160 for adults and NOK80 for children.

Transfers to and from Torp Airport

Ryanair and other budget aircraft' flights land at Sandefjord Airport, Torp in Sandefjord, Norway. In around 110 minutes, the Torp-Expressen bus runs from the airport to the terminal in Galleri Oslo. Buses depart Oslo around 3 ½ hours before the closing of check-in. The buses leave the airport around 35 minutes after the arrival of a flight. However, the bus will wait for the plane that arrives late.

Torp Airport Website
http://www.torp.no/en/frontpage/
Torp Airport Map
https://goo.gl/maps/34XX8XTL2Rz

Torp-Expressen Website
http://torpekspressen.no/
Phone:+47 67 98 04 80

With a cost of NOK266, NSB trains run about every hour between Oslo S and Torp station. A shuttle bus converges with the trains and transports passengers to the airport. The fee for the shuttle ride is included in the train ticket price.

Oslo Pass

The Oslo Pass allows unlimited travel by tram, bus, underground, local train, and boat with NSB and Ruter, within zones 1 and 2. The Pass can also be used to travel to Drøbak (south), Lillestrøm (east), or Asker (west).

Night Buses. The Pass can be used on zones 1 and 2 night buses which run from 1:00 am to 4:00 am on Saturdays and Sundays.

Night Buses Oslo Website
https://ruter.no/en/journey-planner/night-buses/

Tusenfryd Amusement Park. Pass holders have complimentary transport to the amusement park, which is set in zone 2.

Ferries/Boats. The Pass can be used on the boats to Asker, Drøbak, and Nesodden. It can also be used on the ferries going to the Oslo Fjord islands and on the boats to Bygdøy.

Ferries Website
https://ruter.no/en/journey-planner/route-maps/

Ruter

Metro

Ruter is Oslo's main public transport system. It also serves the nearby county of Akershus. Ferries (excluding the Bygdøy ferry), local trains, metro/subway, trams, regional buses, and city buses are included in the Ruter ticket system.

Ruter Website (,trams,Metro,buses,ferries,trains)
https://ruter.no/en/

Tickets can be bought at any Ruter sales point. These places include 7-Eleven and Narvesen shops and metro stations' ticket machines. You should pre-purchase a ticket if you travel by tram or metro/subway.

Single Pre-Bought Ticket
Adult: NOK32
Senior/Child: NOK16

Single Ticket (Purchased from Driver)
Adult: NOK50
Senior/Child: 25NOK
One-Day Ticket
Adult: NOK90
Senior/Child: NOK45

7-Day Ticket
Adult: NOK240
Senior/Child: NOK120

30-Day Ticket
Adult: NOK690
Senior/Child: NOK345

Norwegian Student: NOK414
Year-Round Ticket
Adult: NOK6,900
Senior: NOK3,450

Norwegian State Railways (NSB)

NSB is Norway's national railway company and offers train services in Norway and between Gothenburg, Sweden, and Oslo. Many regional trains have complimentary wireless internet. To use it, however, you need to register.

Norwegian State Railways (NSB) Website
https://www.nsb.no/en/frontpage

The Ferries

Oslo Ferries (Boat to the Islands). The City Hall Pier 4 (Rådhus-brygge 4) boats take you to the inner Oslo Fjord islands. The ferries, during summer, operate from early in the morning to late at night. During winter, there are only 7 to 8 daily departures.

Ruter tickets can be used to board the ferries. However, tickets should be bought in advance as they are not available on the islands.

Bygdøyfergene (Boat to the Museums). You can use the Oslo Pass to board the Bygdøy ferries, which operate from March to October. The ferries depart every 20 to 30 minutes from Pier 3, which is located near City Hall.

One of the ferries' stops is Dronningen, which is the location of Oscarshall, Viking Ship Museum, and Norwegian Museum of Cultural History/Folk Museum). Another stop is Bygdøynes, the location of the Norwegian Maritime Museum, Fram, and Kon-Tiki.

When not using the Oslo Pass, you can buy tickets at Båtservice ticket office at Pier 3. The cost for a one-way ticket is NOK40, and the return ticket is NOK60. If you buy tickets on board, it costs NOK60.

Bicycle Rental

Bicycle Rental Website
http://www.vikingbikingoslo.com/en/
Bicycle Rental Map
https://goo.gl/maps/fCPzY25oAbx
Address:Nedre Slottsgate 4, 0157 Oslo
Phone:+47 412 66 496

59

Top 5 Affordable Hotels

Oslo is a compact city, as compared to capitals of other countries. In the city center, you can reach point A to point B in a relatively short amount of time. From the Oslo Central Station to the Royal Palace (via Karl Johan Street) it will only take about 15 minutes by walking.

If you want to go to the places beyond the city center, you can use public transport and easily reach popular tourist destinations like Bygdøy and Holmenkollen. Using the metro, it takes only 25 minutes to reach Holmenkollen from the city center. During the summer, it takes a 15-minute ferry ride to reach Bygdøy.

Each area in Oslo has unique characteristics. It's also no surprise the city is dotted with hotels, which are strategically located near metro stations so you can reach out-of-the-way destinations in a short amount of time. Some of the best budget hotels in Oslo are listed below.

Oslo Apartments – Sven Bruns Gate

This 3-star hotel/serviced apartment is located in Sven Bruns Gate 7 in Frogner, and is a 10-minute walk away from the Nationaltheatret Tram Station. The hotel is also a family-friendly serviced apartment.

Throughout the property, guests can enjoy the complimentary wireless internet. Each of the apartments features an in-room dining area, a coffee maker, and a refrigerator. The apartments also have ironing facilities, flat screen TVs, and seating areas.

The area where the hotel's at is known for its vibrant nightlife. Guests are spoilt for choice when it comes to bar and dining options. The Oslo Apartments – Sven Bruns Gate is also near the Homansbyen Light Rail Station, making it easy for visitors explore the city and the surrounding vicinity. Also near the hotel are Bislett Stadion and Oslo City Hall.

Oslo Apartments – Sven Bruns Gate Website
http://osloapartments.no/en/apartments-for-rent/
oslo-central/sven-bruns-gate-7.html

Oslo Apartments – Sven Bruns Gate Map
https://goo.gl/maps/KE422GisX5R2
Address: Sven Bruns gate 7, 0166 Oslo, Norway
Phone:(+47) 22 51 02 50

Radisson Blu Plaza Hotel Oslo

This stylish 4-star hotel is located at Sonja Henies Plass 3 in Sentrum. The hotel is also set amid various boutiques and shops, and is minutes away from Bussterminalen Oslo.

As a guest, you can enjoy a sauna and an indoor pool. The hotel is also close to bars and clubs, and you can explore easily the local nightlife. One well-known landmark is the Oslo Spektrum, which is only a few meters away from the hotel. Radisson Blu Plaza Hotel Oslo is also within walking distance of the Oslo Opera House, Karl Johans gate, and Stortinget.

Radisson Blu Plaza Hotel Oslo Website
https://www.radissonblu.com/en/plazahotel-oslo
Radisson Blu Plaza Hotel Oslo Map
https://goo.gl/maps/gKDsbrHTYcn
Address: Sonja Henies Plass 3, 0185 Oslo
Phone:+47 22 05 80 00

Saga Poshtel Oslo Central

This 2-star hostel is a pleasantly surprising gem located in Kongens Gate 7 in Sentrum. It's a 10-minute walk away from the Oslo Central Station and is strategically located in the city center.

Even with its 2-star accommodations, the hostel nevertheless has a lot to offer its guests including: complimentary Wi-Fi, luggage storage, and 24-hour reception. A communal living room is an excellent place to meet fellow international travelers. The hostel offers guests a buffet breakfast, and it also has a shared kitchen.

Nearby attractions include Stortinget, Karl Johans gate, Nationaltheatret Tram Station, and Aker Brygge.

Saga Poshtel Oslo Central Website
http://www.sagahoteloslocentral.no/
Saga Poshtel Oslo Central Map
https://goo.gl/maps/bC7iHJvfmRK2
Address: Kongens gate 7, 0153 Oslo
Phone:+47 23 10 08 00

The Apartments Company – Parkveien

Located in Parkveien 4, The Apartments Company is a five-minute walk away from the Homansbyen Light Rail Station. It's also a short stroll away from Palace Park, the Royal Palace, and Bislett Stadion.

The Gardermoen airport is 45 minutes away by car, and Nationaltheatret Tram Station is a short walk away. Also within walking distance are the Christiania Theatre, the Nationaltheatret, and the National Museum of Art, Architecture, and Design.

The Apartments Company – Parkveien Website
http://www.theapartmentscompany.no/
The Apartments Company – Parkveien Map
https://goo.gl/maps/3G1pr5pEm10
Address:0195 Oslo, Norway
Phone:+47 22 69 04 50

Thon Hotel Rosenkratz Oslo

This 4-star hotel is located at the Rosenkrantz Gate 1 in Sentrum, and offers a concierge, meeting rooms, and a 24-hour reception. Guests can access a fitness center. The hotel's contemporary rooms include newspapers and wireless Internet access.

There is also a bar and a restaurant where guests can relax after a busy day of touring the Oslo surroundings. From this hotel, you can easily discover the city's best offerings. Thon Hotel Rosenkrantz Oslo is located near the Nationaltheatret, the Oslo City Hall, and the People's Theatre. Oslo Spektrum is a short walk away.

Thon Hotel Rosenkratz Oslo Website
http://www.theapartmentscompany.no/
Thon Hotel Rosenkratz Oslo Map
https://goo.gl/maps/Dgr28RMcQ7N2
Address: Rosenkrantz' gate 1, 0159
Phone:+47 23 31 55 00

60

Exploring the Bars in Helsinki: Top 5 Bars

The focus of Helsinki bars is on locally brewed and imported **ales**. For centuries, it has worked, and locals are satisfied. Though the process of producing ales is rather complex, bars in Helsinki prefer to serve them.

Main reason? For them, these are flavorful beyond compare.

Is It a Good Idea to Go to a Bar?

Yes, it's a good idea to go to a bar. It's one of the best places to unwind.

Since many bartenders in Helsinki are very accommodating, you can talk about your day to someone who's all ears. While you enjoy a flavorful glass of your chosen beer, you can narrate tales and be as detailed as you wish.

If you don't have money on hand to pay for your drinks, don't fret. Most of the bars in the city accept cards. In fact, these places prefer payment via credit or debit card.

If you want to celebrate a fulfilling day around the city with a glass of beer, you can do so. In Helsinki, you have plenty of options!

Top five bars:

(1)Musta Kissa

Musta Kissa (or The Black Cat) is a bar where you can chill and discover local Helsinki culture. It's designed with 1960s and 1970s Finnish furniture. There, you can enjoy beer and engage in worthwhile conversation.

Phone:+358 40 7711785
Address:15 Toinen Iinja
Musta Kissa Website
http://www.barmustakissa.fi/
Musta Kissa Map
https://goo.gl/maps/fmpdw8uvNzm

(2)Bar Bäkkäri

Bar Bäkkäri is a venue that provides a hard rock vibe. Its walls are decorated with rock memorabilia of sorts – artworks, signed records, and tour posters. On weekends, it features live gigs.

Address:21 Pohjoinen Rautatiekatu
Bar Bäkkäri Website
http://www.bakkari.fi/
Bar Bäkkäri Map
https://goo.gl/maps/wGdVqRiCBHP2

(3)Liberty or Death

To have a taste of Finland's finest cocktails, Liberty or Death is the bar to go to. The place is quite small and it's dimly lit. Because of its intimate environment, you can relax as desired.

Phone:+358505424870
Address: 6 Erottajankatu
Liberty or Death Website
https://www.facebook.com/pages/Liberty-Or-Death
/297266020341987
Liberty or Death Map
https://goo.gl/maps/MnQWzhFJ6MR2

(4)Bar Molotow

A "respectable" bar in Helsinki is Bar Molotow. The place features enjoyable indie, punk, and rock music. With a Scandinavian functionalist design as its theme, it's a happy place for many young rockers.

Phone:+358 40 1234567
Address: 29 Vaasankatu
Bar Molotow Website
https://www.facebook.com/
Bar-Molotow-156875074356672/
Bar Molotow Map
https://goo.gl/maps/3H7ZbKhkrL92

(5)Siltanen

Siltanen is a bar that displays a live gig venue. It's a great place to hang out in because it offers fairly priced menus. It features local and international musicians who play tracks of different genres.

Phone:+358 44 0660530
Address: 13 B Hameentie
Siltanen Website
http://www.siltanen.org/siltanen/

Siltanen Map
https://goo.gl/maps/ZfA6JFJEJE72

61

Top 5 Restaurants

The culinary scene is a Scandinavian gem, and features everything from freshly-caught fish to succulent reindeer. While there are a number of restaurants in the city, listed below are five of the best Oslo restaurants.

Café Engebret

The restaurant is considered the oldest restaurant in Oslo. You get to experience old world charm with draped curtains, wood paneling, and candlelight. The traditional food changes with the seasons, and it's like the food is prepared in a way that is similar to centuries past.

Seafood is served in the spring, reindeer is a constant offering, and fresh cod can be enjoyed in January. While you dine, you can imagine Grieg, Ibsen, and other Nordic greats ate at the restaurant during its 150-year history.

Café Engebret Website
http://engebret-cafe.no/
Café Engebret Map
https://goo.gl/maps/UtPtZSim1LN2
Address: Bankplassen 1
Contact Number: +47 22 82 25 25

Ekebergrestauranten

When visiting Oslo, expect to be entranced by the incomparable vistas and fjords. They are only some of the things that Ekeber-grestauranten has to offer. At the restaurant, you can enjoy the beautiful landscapes and Oslo's natural panorama.

You can choose to eat at the veranda, the outdoor restaurant, the café, the private chamber, and the classy dining room. At the restaurant, you are offered the chance to see the majesty of Oslo. You can take in the sights of the glorious city over a quality dish and a glass of wine.

Ekebergrestauranten Website
http://www.ekebergrestauranten.com/
Ekebergrestauranten Map

https://goo.gl/maps/Cvsh7wFv8Xs
Address: Kongsvelen 15
Contact Number: +47 2324 2300

Maaemo

It's not only a restaurant; Maaemo is also a dining experience. The owners suggest that diners allocate an entire evening to appreciate and savor fully the set menu, which is a selection of simplistic reductions and raw foods that add up to 26 plates.

The dining experience can last an entire evening, and wine pairings are chosen carefully to bring out each ingredient's flavor. While spruce juice, reindeer heart, mead gel, and fried rye-bread cream may sound fabricated, they are actually true dishes served in pleasant visual arrangements.

Maaemo Website
https://maaemo.no/
Maaemo Map
https://goo.gl/maps/VsBxHjtXaSA2
Address: Schweigaards gate 15b
Contact Number: +47 9199 4805

Madu

The restaurant is located in the boutique First Hotel Grims Grenka. The restaurant is a traditional Scandinavian restaurant that special-izes in seasonal raw food and thrives on the imagination of the chef.

The dishes are cooked at low temperatures or served raw to preserve their subtleties and flavor. The food served loses none of the original goodness and organic nature encased within the ingredients' molecules. The ingredients, mainly seafood and fish, are often smoked, pickled, mixed with contrasting flavors, or cured.

Madu Map
https://goo.gl/maps/hAFG7xARHtj
Address: Kongens gate 5
Contact Number: +47 2310 7200

Markveien Mat og Vinhus

The restaurant chefs use ingredients that are bought from the best local sources. Fresh, locally-grown produce goes into traditional dishes, with lamb, oxtail, and crayfish appearing on the menu. The only thing that makes the ingredients un-Norwegian is the terrine, which is of French origin. The dining room is also of the French style.

Markveien Mat og Vinhus Website
http://www.markveien.no/
Markveien Mat og Vinhus Map
https://goo.gl/maps/S97RP35gt6M2
Address: Torkbajj gate 12
Contact Number: +47 2237 2297

62

Best Famous Oslo City Landmarks

In terms of land area, Oslo is one of the world's largest capital cities. However, only 20 percent of the city's area has been developed; the rest consists of protected forests, parks, numerous lakes, and hills. Open spaces and parks are integral to the cityscape, and can be accessed easily from any part of the city.

The Oslo city center can be explored on foot, as the center has many pedestrian-friendly areas, like Karl Johans gate. Consistently ranked as one of the world's best cities to live in, Oslo is rich in culture and known for its theaters, galleries, and museums. Some of the five best famous Oslo landmarks are listed below.

Aker Brygge

The Aker Brygge area, which is constructed around an abandoned shipyard, is the city's heart and soul. The visually-stunning landmark draws in around 12 million visitors annually. Visitors are drawn by the great restaurants, fine shopping, seafront boardwalk, and patio bars with their fireplaces and snug rugs.

While at Aker Brygge, you can visit the Astrup Fearnley Museum of Modern Art, which houses works by artists Damien Hirst, Jeff Koons, and Andy Warhol, among other contemporary artists.

Location: Bryggegata 9, 0120
Aker Brygge Website
https://www.akerbrygge.no/english/
Aker Brygge Map
https://goo.gl/maps/34yGPqDHRhH2

Akershus Fortress

The fortress rises above the Oslo fjord and sits on the promontory of Akershes. The Akershus Fortress was constructed under the reign of Haakon V. Explore the ramparts and the grounds and then explore the chapel with the tomb of Haakon VII. Also tour the original

357

medieval castle's remains.

Located in the fortress's grounds is the Museum of Norwegian Resistance, and spend a few hours knowing more about the German occupation in Norway during World War II.

Location: Akershus Festning, 0015

Akershus Fortress Website
http://www.forsvarsbygg.no/festningene/Festningene
/Akershus-festning/English/
Akershus Fortress Map
https://goo.gl/maps/GNf5MaPSJhH2
Phone:+47 23 09 39 17

Oslo Opera House

With its unique contemporary architecture, the Oslo Opera House is home to the National Opera Theatre and the Norwegian National Opera and Ballet. With its 1,364 seating capacity, the architectural wonder is designed to create the effect that it's slipping into the harbor.

The opera house is also the country's largest cultural building since the 14th century Nidaros Cathedral in Trondheim. As a visitor, you can also join various tours and public programs. Delight also in a stroll on the inclining roof.

Location: Kirsten Flagstads Plass 1, 0150

Oslo Opera House Website
http://operaen.no/
Oslo Opera House Map
https://goo.gl/maps/MULaaQnkcaR2
Phone: +47 21 42 21 21

Royal Palace

Set high on Karl Johans gate's northwest end, the Norwegian Royal Palace is a prominent sight in the city's landscape. The 173-room palace is closed to the public, but visitors can watch the regular changing of the guard on the grounds. They are also free to wander the gardens and grounds. Close by is the Norwegian Nobel Institute.

Location: Bellevue
Royal Palace Website
https://goo.gl/xGLxGD
Royal Palace Map
https://goo.gl/maps/VFt3GQXXyJ92
Phone:+47 22 04 87 00

Vigeland Sculpture Park

The park, which is the largest of its kind in the world, is a famed tourist attraction. The sculpture park, which is open year round, features the works of Gustav Vigeland and contains 650 of his sculptures in wrought iron, granite, and bronze.

In the park, which was completed in 1949, Vigeland took part in the park's layout and design, placing most of the works in five groups along an axis that spans 2,800 feet. The fountain group is the oldest, depicting the human life's cycle.

Location: Nobels gate 32, N-0268

Vigeland Sculpture Park Website
http://www.vigeland.museum.no/no/vigelandsparken
Vigeland Sculpture Park Map
https://goo.gl/maps/GA9s7tjTPPJ2
Phone:+47 23 49 37 00

63

Best Museums

If you love art and you seek to know about cultures other than your own, a visit to Oslo is well worth it, as the city has more than 50 museums. With an art tour of the past and present of Norway's capital, you get to see how Oslo has defined itself as an artistic center in Scandinavia. Below are five of the best museums that the city of Oslo has to offer locals and visitors.

<u>Holmenkollen Ski Museum & Tower</u>

As a historical Norwegian landmark, Holmenkollen represents over a century of skiing competitions. Within the ski jump is the Holmenkollen Ski Museum, which presents over four millennia of skiing history.

The museum also showcases exhibitions on modern skiing and snowboarding and Norwegian polar exploration antiquities. On top of the jump tower is the observation deck, which offers sweeping city views. Open year round, the museum also has a shop, café, and ski simulator.

Address: Kongeveien 5, 0787
Phone:+47 916 71 947

Holmenkollen Ski Museum & Tower Website
http://www.skiforeningen.no/holmenkollen
Holmenkollen Ski Museum & Tower Map
https://goo.gl/maps/LDKeg9tcFet

Munch Museum

The museum, also called Munchmuseet, boasts of the world's largest collection of the works of Edvard Munch. The collection provides insight into Munch as an Expressionism pioneer. The artist bequeathed to the city his collection of paintings, drawings, and graphical prints.

Address: Tøyengata 53, 0578
Phone:+47 23 49 35 00

Munch Museum Website
http://munchmuseet.no/
Munch Museum Map
https://goo.gl/maps/FGQwrf5xVf82

National Gallery

Established in 1837, the National Gallery contains Norway's largest public collection of drawings, paintings, and sculpture. The central attractions of the gallery include Edvard Munch's Madonna and The Scream, and paintings by Manet and Cézanne.

The museum's permanent collection highlights works from the Romantic period until the mid-1900s. Other works exhibited are the art of international sculptors and painters. The Fairy Tale Room has art depicting fairy tale creatures like princesses, fairies, and trolls. Admission is free with the Oslo Pass.

Address: Universitetsgata 13, 0164
Phone:+47 21 98 20 00

National Gallery Website
http://www.nasjonalmuseet.no/
National Gallery Map
https://goo.gl/maps/5X2qHiNNKDD2

National Museum – Architecture

The museum explores historical and contemporary themes through photographs, drawings, and models. Designed by Christian Heinrich Grosch, the main building was completed in 1830. After an extension and a renovation by Sverre Fehn, the building started to be used as a museum in 2008.

The building is a juxtaposition of modernist architecture and classicism. It's an encounter between Fehn and Grosch, who are Norway's most important architects of the 20th and 19th centuries, respectively.

Address: Universitetsgata 13, 0164
Phone:+47 21 98 20 00

National Museum – Architecture Website
http://www.nasjonalmuseet.no/
National Museum – Architecture Map
https://goo.gl/maps/F4g9Up3xGFo

The Kon-Tiki Museum

Norwegian ethnographer and adventurer Thor Heyerdahl became famous when, in 1947, he crossed the Pacific Ocean on the Kon-Tiki raft. He then had subsequent expeditions on the reed boats Tigris and Ra.

At the museum, guests can see the original vessels and exhibits on Heyerdahl's expeditions, including Kon-Tiki, Tigris, Ra, Galapagos, Tucume, Fatu-Hiva, Easter Island, Thor Heyerdahl's library, Tiki pop culture, Thor Heyerdahl the person, and underwater exhibit, and a 30-meter cave tour.

Address: Bygdøynesveien 36, 0286
Phone:+47 23 08 67 67

The Kon-Tiki Museum Website
http://www.kon-tiki.no/
The Kon-Tiki Museum Map
https://goo.gl/maps/eFgCb9iDv1G2

64

Best Art Galleries

While Oslo is smaller compared to other international art centers, it's still reputed for its specialist auction houses and galleries. The city's art galleries offer visitors the chance to know more about Norway's art history. They also provide insight for individuals who seek to invest in art while in Oslo.

Astrup Fearnley Museet

The Astrup Fearnley Collection comprises contemporary and modern art that are considered significant in Northern Europe. The museum changes up its collection by rotating exhibits of well-known artists with its permanent collection.

Renowned architect Renzo Piano designed the gallery, and is comprised of 3 pavilions that rest under a uniquely-shaped glass roof. The building is inspired by its maritime environment.

Address: Strandpromenaden 2, 0252
Phone:+47 22 93 60 60

Astrup Fearnley Museet Website
http://www.afmuseet.no/
Astrup Fearnley Museet Map

https://goo.gl/maps/h4Z4U46GbQz

Blomqvist Auction House Gallery

Established in 1870, Blomqvist is the country's largest and oldest auction house. The gallery deals in Norwegian antiques and art, and is considered an Edvard Munch expert.

Aside from paintings, photographs, prints, and sculptures, the gallery also specializes and deals in silver, furniture, china, country antiques, glass, oriental items, and jewelry.

Address: Tordenskiolds gate 5
Phone:+47 22 70 87 70

Blomqvist Auction House Gallery Website
https://www.blomqvist.no/
Blomqvist Auction House Gallery Map
https://goo.gl/maps/fdBCn8sqZtp

Galleri Heer

Galleri Heer was established at its current address in 1986. However, the gallery's history goes back to 1981 when Olav Postmyr opened the gallery in Drøbak.

Galleri Heer is a contemporary art gallery that exhibits the works of various artists: old and young, female and male, and veterans and debutants. The gallery showcases mostly artistic expressions, including photography, drawing, graphics, and sculpture.

Address: Seilduksgata 4, 0553
Phone:+47 22 38 54 32

Galleri Heer Website
http://www.galleriheer.no/
Galleri Heer Map
https://goo.gl/maps/y3GXZ1MdHq62

Museum of Contemporary Art

The Museum of Contemporary Art has four permanent installations, including gallery rooms that are allocated for the works of Louis Bourgeois. The gallery also has a permanent collection of 5,000 works by international and Norwegian artists.

The museum gallery's collection also covers a wide spectrum of media and genres: print-making, paintings, photography, drawing, objects, sculpture, video art, and installation. The gallery offers guided tours in Norwegian every Sunday, and guided tours in English during the summer.

Address: Bankplassen 4, 0151
Phone:+47 21 98 20 00
Museum of Contemporary Art Website
http://www.nasjonalmuseet.no/en/
Museum of Contemporary Art Map
https://goo.gl/maps/kS43YsYTanv

The Queen Joséphine Gallery

The gallery opens during the summer and is open to all Oscarshall visitors. Located in Oscarshall's museum shop annex, the gallery showcases classic Norwegian art.

The gallery is named for Queen Joséphine, who is King Oscar I's mother. Both the king and queen were interested in art, and they laid the groundwork for the classic Norwegian art collection at the Royal Palace today.

Address: Oscarshallveien, 0287
Phone:+47 917 02 361

The Queen Joséphine Gallery Website
http://www.royalcourt.no/artikkel.html?tid=117403
The Queen Joséphine Gallery Map
https://goo.gl/maps/UBLA23fLET62

65

Best Coffee Shops

Oslo has a high standard of living, and residents seek to have the right work-life balance. Oslo's residents also love a good cup of coffee. Below are some of the city's best places to sip a cup of coffee and bite into a delectable pastry.

Alfred

Alfred's head chef, Joni Leskinen, used the success of eco-restaurants as his inspiration for the café. For food preparation, Alfred utilizes only sustainable and locally-sourced produce. Patrons can choose to sit outdoors on the patio or inside the cafe. One of the most highly recommended food items is Alfred's open-faced shrimp sandwich.

Address: Brynjulf Bulls Plass 1, 0250
Phone:+47 400 06 611
Alfred Map
https://goo.gl/maps/VmJukuLwt292

Café Amsterdam

Café Amsterdam is Norway's first Dutch café, and it gives off an authentic Dutch vibe. The café is relaxing and cozy by day, and a dynamic and vibrant pub at night. The artwork and décor all come from the Netherlands, and the traditional snacks let you catch a sneak peek of Dutch cuisine. A must-try dish is bitterballen – a deep fried meatball.

Address: Kristian Augusts Gate 12, 0164
Phone:+47 401 69 089

Café Amsterdam Website
http://cafeamsterdam.no/
Café Amsterdam Map
https://goo.gl/maps/EiJyxJ6Lo8N2

Café Celsius

Café Celsius is your best hangout if you seek an afternoon appreciating Norwegian buildings rich in history. Set in Christiania Square, the café is close to a number of the city's oldest buildings. The vanilla-marinated strawberry is a must-try and the desserts and coffee are outstanding. The outdoor sitting area tends to be crowded during summer.

Address: Rådhusgata 19, 0158
Phone:+47 22 42 45 39
Café Celsius Website
http://www.kafecelsius.no/
Café Celsius Map
https://goo.gl/maps/aiX5E6zXrW72

Grosch

Grosch is a great place to have lunch and it's also a fine venue for hangouts and meetings. Grosch is set right next to the National Museum of Architecture, which was built as Norges Banks in 1828. Guests at Grosch can partake of a relaxing meal beside the historic structure. Some of the recommended desserts served in the café are mousse, waffles, and sweet passionfruit panna cotta.

Address: Bankplassen 3 0151
Phone:+47 22 42 12 12

Grosch Website
http://www.groschbistro.no/
Grosch Map
https://goo.gl/maps/DjHR7ontMpJ2

66

Top 5 Bars

Oslo is known for its relaxing work environment. Moreover, visitors to Oslo can see the sights during the day, and unwind at night. As for locals, they can have a nightcap after a hard day's work. Below are five of the best bars in the city.

Brooms & Hatchets

Brooms & Hatchets offers you an authentic Norwegian way to

drink and enjoy a night out. The bar is known to bring out the best in Norwegian culture and identity to its guests. The classy yet modern bar has a superb atmosphere, and the local craftsmanship is showcased flawlessly in the Nordic gastro-pub food and local beers. You can also choose from a variety of spirits and cocktails.

Address: Kongens gate 5, 0153
Phone:+47 23 10 72 00
Brooms & Hatches Website
https://www.facebook.com/broomsandhatchets/

Etoile Bar

Rooftop bars are popular during the summer, and they are an excellent option if you want to enjoy a drink. Set on the Grand Hotel's eighth floor, Etoile Bar allows you to catch a scenic view of the Oslo skyline as well as of Karl Johans gate. At night, the bar becomes vibrant and energetic. The roof terrace is open during good weather.

Address: Karl Johans Gate 31, 0159
Phone:+47 23 21 20 00
Etoile Bar Website
http://www.grand.no/no/restaurantandbar/
eight-rooftop-bar.html
Etoile Bar Map
https://goo.gl/maps/XwH1hkJqt3F2

Internasjonalen

Opened in 2003, Internasjonalen is one of the city's best drinking spots. The bar utilizes the functionalist style of Eastern Europe as the décor's main theme, paying homage to the long working class tradition. Internasjonalen serves a variety of wines, snacks, cocktails, and rare spirits. From time to time, live music performances are also held. You can be entertained the entire evening with an eclectic playlist.

Address: Youngstorget 2 A, 0181
Phone:+47 468 25 240
Internasjonalen Website
http://www.internasjonalen.no/
Internasjonalen Map
https://goo.gl/maps/brAhp18Apsv

Izakaya

Izakaya, which is a Japanese pub, offers you a unique drinking experience. The bar brings you a real Japanese drinking experience, as the izakaya culture has been popular in the Asian country for many years. The furnishings and décor stay true to izakaya. Also served are Japanese beers, wines, sake, and spirits.

Address: St. Olavs Gate 7 0165
Phone:+47 463 45 679
Izakaya Website
http://izakayaoslo.com/
Izakaya Map
https://goo.gl/maps/yEMoUThYWxv

Tosca Bar

Tosca Bar, which is set on the Thon Hotel Opera's ground floor, is a popular place to enjoy light drinks and refreshments. Comfortable, colorful chairs paired with exquisite bar tables create a dynamic atmosphere for the bar patrons. Light snacks and small dishes are also served, and many of them are meant to complement your cocktail or glass of wine. Veteran mixologists prepare the cocktails, and you can make your own cocktail, too.

Address: Dronning Eufemias Gate 4, 0191
Phone:+47 24 10 30 00

Tosca Bar Website
https://www.thonhotels.no/hoteller/norge/
oslo/thon-hotel-opera/
Tosca Bar Map
https://goo.gl/maps/2j9hXds3uSk

67

Top 5 Nightclubs

Norwegians are usually not big on social drinking. With residents becoming more cosmopolitan, however, Oslo's nightscape continually offers a wider array of nightlife choices. Tourists prefer the British-style pubs, and live jazz has also found its corner. Young professionals are drawn to clubs that let them dance and enjoy listening to live music. Below are 5 of Oslo's top nightclubs.

Blå

Blå is a nightclub for contemporary jazz, live, R&B, hip-hop, and related sounds. It's also a venue that welcomes upcoming acts from around Norway. International artists perform here as well. Concerts are held during the early evenings, while the place turns into a vibrant nightclub well into the night, where Norwegian and international DJs work their magic.

Address: Brenneriveien 9 C, 0182

Blå Website
http://www.blaaoslo.no/kontakt/
Blå Map
https://goo.gl/maps/gbuFiT5WECo

Hard Rock Café Oslo

Hard Rock Café Oslo is a nightclub, bar, and restaurant that fuses contemporary Scandinavian design with vibrant rock n' roll, good food, and classic Hard Rock style. The nightclub and café is open year round, and its walls are covered with famous musicians' rock n' roll memorabilia.

The nightclub and café boasts of more than 30 flat-screens, a stage, and a superb sound system, making it an ideal venue for various events. Moreover, the party atmosphere of the nightclub lasts into the wee hours.

Address: Karl Johans gate 45, 0162
Phone:+47 400 06 260

Hard Rock Café Oslo Website
http://www.hardrockcafe.no/
Hard Rock Café Oslo Map
https://goo.gl/maps/7FbBbCJqLzr

Revolver

This rock arena has a restaurant, a cocktail bar, and a basement bar that holds club nights and concerts. Mission Taco, which is Revolver's restaurant, serves affordable Mexican street food. The bar is open daily and the minimum age to enter is 23 years old. The nightclub's minimum entrance age is 20 years old.

Address: Møllergata 32, 0179
Phone:+47 22 20 22 32

Revolver Website

https://www.revolveroslo.no/
Revolver Map
https://goo.gl/maps/KSymx1TVMXk

Skaugum

At Skaugum's special atmosphere, you get to enjoy good music and a proper backyard. Open year round, Skaugum offers shade during summers and heating cables, heat lamps, hot drinks, an open grill, and dancing during colder days.

The unique nightclub has 3 floors, with 50 sinks bolted to walls and an unexpected music profile. Concerts are regularly held during summers. Concerts are also held at the bar year round. Skaugum is also a popular weekend nightclub, attracting guests from around town.

Address: Solligata 2, 0254
Phone:+47 23 13 11 40

Skaugum Website
http://palacegrill.no/
Skaugum Map
https://goo.gl/maps/8Gj74MikBPL2

The Villa

The Villa is an electronica club that is highly rated among its guests. The nightclub plays underground music like techno, house, drum 'n' bass, dubstep, electro, and other musical genres.

The nightclub consists of two dance floors. The weekends feature international and Norwegian DJs, artists, and live acts. Guests have to be at least 23 years old to enter the nightclub. However, guests

20-22 years of age may be able to enter so long as they send a prior email to the club.

Address: Møllergata 23, 0179
Phone:+47 932 55 745

The Villa Website
http://www.thevilla.no/
The Villa Map
https://goo.gl/maps/ynJ6qVUj2XQ2

68

Unique or Special Activities You can do Only in Oslo

Oslo is indeed of the world's most beautiful cities. It's also a great place to know more about and experience Nordic culture. Moreover, there are also a few things that can only be experienced in Oslo. Below are some of the unique things, underground activities, alternative sights, and hidden gems that you can enjoy.

Flea Markets

If you want a unique and authentic Oslo experience, it's a good idea to go to a thrift shop or flea market. The city has at least seven flea markets, but the most recommended go-to markets are Blå and Birkelunden flea market.

Birkelunden sells mainly vintage books, jewelry, and furniture. Blå sells second-hand items and handicrafts like glass, ceramics, paintings, bags, and wool. Here, you can also meet the local designers and artists, and their inspiring artistic perception.

Notable Flea Market Addresses:
Brenneriveien 9 C, 0182
https://goo.gl/maps/epp5ZciCuLJ2
Grünerløkka 0552
https://goo.gl/maps/uX7BB6xq7K82

Music Festivals

Concert venues are everywhere, as Norwegians love their local and international music. Oslo's largest music festival is Øya Festival, which takes place yearly during August. The festival attracts over 60,000 music lovers to Medieval Park.

If you can't chance upon the Øya Festival, there are other spectacular live music performances in the city. Mono, Blå, and Rockefeller have the most cutting-edge sound systems and the more popular bands.

Here, you can enjoy listening to folk music or heavy metal:

Blå
Address:Brenneriveien 9, 0182
Blå Website

http://www.blaaoslo.no/kontakt/
Bla Map
https://goo.gl/maps/dr7NyG3dwT72

Mono
Address: Pløens Gate 4, 0181
Mono Website
http://www.cafemono.no/
Mono Map
https://goo.gl/maps/pPurYmKUHsR2

Rockefeller
Address:Torggata 16, 0181
Rockefeller Website
http://www.rockefeller.no/
Rockefeller Map
https://goo.gl/maps/Egn3sogH2SN2

Norwegian Architecture

Architecture enthusiasts would find Oslo a paradise. Norwegian architecture's new direction has dramatically changed the city's landscape. From modern styles to medieval structures, there are many buildings that are worth a visit. Futuristic streamlined designs characterize the Holmenkollen Ski Jump and ZipLine. The unique Mortensrud Church integrates nature with slate glass.

Notable Architecture:

Mortensrud Website
https://kirken.no/kirkeneioslo
Mortensrud Church Map
https://goo.gl/maps/fTnv5bkhiP72
Address:Helga Vaneks vei 15, 1281
Phone:+47 23 62 99 80

Holmenkollen Ski Jump and ZipLine Website
http://www.skiforeningen.no/holmenkollen
Holmenkollen Ski Jump and ZipLine Map
https://goo.gl/maps/FviCwbLiMgA2
Address: Kongeveien 5, 0787
Phone:+47 22 92 32 00

Østmarka Wilderness Area

Østmarka, which is set east of Oslo, is unique as its vegetation and geology are markedly different from other forests in the surroundings.

During summer, you can go biking, hiking, and swimming or fishing in the lake. You can also delight in some of the Arctic animals and plants. During winter, you can watch the aurora borealis that skirts the city or ski on the trails. At Østmarka, you get to appreciate Oslo's priceless beauty.

Location: Østmarka, 0687

Østmarka Wilderness Area Map
https://goo.gl/maps/AQqEPxqt95o

Street Art

Graffiti, murals, and paintings can be found all over Oslo. You can find art in a wall's tiny corner next to a garbage bin. Street art may entirely cover a building's whole wall. There are also artists working on street art projects.

Oslo-based artists Pøbel and Dolk, for example, have worked on the 'Living Decay' project, which pertains to a derelict house in the Lofoten Archipelago.

69

Safety While Traveling in Oslo

When you visit Oslo, you are guaranteed of your safety. However, you shouldn't let your guard down and throw caution to the wind. Anything can still happen, and you still must take precautions when going to another country.

Generally, crimes against tourists in Oslo and the rest of Norway are rare, and crime rates are normally low. Crimes that involve violence are somewhat unheard of. Public transport that is generally used by tourists is deemed safe. It's common sense, though, to keep an eye on your valuables in crowded areas in order to prevent problems that might occur.

A reason that Oslo may be safe can be attributed to the longer daylight hours. During the busy summer travel months, it's only dark between 12 midnight and 4 in the morning. During the darker hours, even a bit of light can still filter through. It is agreed in general that crime is likely to happen during the dark, which is not a conducive factor in the city.

Not all places in the city are tourist-friendly, though. You may want to steer clear of the area west/south of the Central Station. The area is deemed to be the city's drug-dealing sector. It's also considered the city's seedier area. While that area is normally safe, you don't have to go there if you don't have a specific reason.

Since 2009, prostitution has been declared illegal in Norway.
Oslo has excellent hygiene and health standards. You can drink the tap water, which is considered high quality.

Phone Police:112
Phone Ambulance:113

70

3-Day Travel Itinerary

Oslo is a paradox – a city set in the countryside. While Oslo is one of the largest European capitals in terms of land area (450 square kilometers), its population is quite small – with only 1.5 million inhabitants.

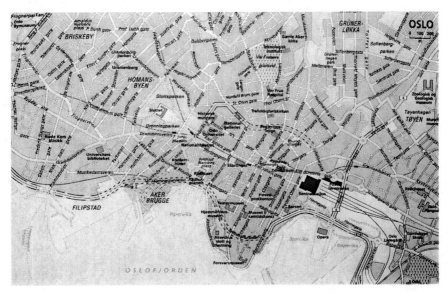

Thus, if you have enjoyed the shops, galleries, cafes, and bars, you can easily slip on to a train or bicycle, into a kayak or yacht, or into ice skates or skis and explore the great outdoors. You can do that without leaving Oslo's land area. Below is one suggested itinerary that lets you explore the rural and urban area of Oslo in three days.

Oslo Kayak Tours Website
http://www.oslokayaktours.no/
Phone: +47 95368249

First Day: Exploring Oslo by Land

Oslo was established in 1048, and razed to the ground in 1624. Because of the natural and man-made changes that were done to the city, modern-day Oslo is now an eclectic mix of new and old culture and architecture. Oslo is the city that inspired Edvard Munch the artist and Henrik Ibsen the playwright.

Start your day by feeling this cultural and diverse city on a sight-seeing tour. Go to the land-based city museums and know more about Viking history. Also visit the art galleries and folk museums. A must-see attraction is the Vigeland Sculpture Park.

Second Day: Exploring Oslo by Sea

Oslo is situated at the Oslo Fjord's head. Ride a ferry boat and take in the vibrant scenery. Enjoy looking at the inlets, islands, and the Akershus Fortress that had once defended the city from foreign attacks.

If you want to explore Oslo by land and sea, take the bus/boat tour that includes the maritime museum. Go for the Oslo experience if you want to see the museums, fjords, the Holmenkollen Ski Jump, and the Kon-Tiki Raft. With this tour, you get to experience the countryside, fjord, and city in one go.

Third Day: Exploring Oslo in Detail

Contemporary Oslo has a lot to offer you if you seek the time to enjoy the sights. Board the Hop-On, Hop-Off Bus and take a look at the cosmopolitan city's shops and cafes. You can also pretend to be a Viking and visit the Viking Ship Museum.

You can also go to the Nobel Peace Centre and commemorate the achievements of individuals who seek to make the world a better place. You can also visit the Munch Museum and see the works of Norway's most famous painter.

Nobel Peace Center Website
https://www.nobelpeacecenter.org/en/
Nobel Peace Center Map
https://goo.gl/maps/Khiy9SzuH9E2
Phone:+47 48 30 10 00

With the Oslo Pass, you can access 33 attractions and museums. As the sun sets, you can take a cruise on a conventional wooden ship and imagine you're Thor Heyerdahl.

Here's another three–day itinerary.

First Day

Buy shrimp off the shrimp boats at the harbor fronting the town hall (Rådhus), and ride a ferry over to the Bygdøy peninsula, which houses some of the city's major museums that are within walking distance of each other.

Explore Fram (the polar ship), the Viking ships, the Norwegian Maritime Museum, the Norwegian Folk Museum, and the Kon-Tiki Museum. In the afternoon, visit the Vigeland Sculpture Park in Frognerpark.

Second Day

Use this day for the Frommer's walking tour, and enjoy your lunch at a traditional Norwegian restaurant. Visit the Edvard Munch Museum in the afternoon. During summer, indulge in some fresh air and beer at the Studenter Lunden, which is close to the National Theatre.

Third Day

In the morning, take another Frommer's walking tour, and have lunch along your tour. After lunch, tour the Akershus Fortress and the nearby Norwegian Resistance Museum.

Late in the afternoon, go to the Tryvannstårnet lookout tower and the Holmenkollen Ski Museum, where you can enjoy sweeping Oslo views. You can also eat dinner at Holmenkollen.

--

Indeed, Oslo is a wonderful city that has it all: winter and summer, outdoor and indoor, sea and land. Your only concern is that how you'll explore the city in just three days.

71

Conclusion

I want to thank you for reading this book! I sincerely hope that you received value from it!

If you received value from this book, I want to ask you for a favour.Would you be kind enough to leave a review for this book on Amazon?

This document is geared towards providing exact and reliable information in regards to the topic and issue covered. The publication is sold with the idea that the publisher is not required to render accounting, officially permitted, or otherwise, qualified services. If advice is necessary, legal or professional, a practiced individual in the profession should be ordered.

- From a Declaration of Principles which was accepted and approved equally by a Committee of the American Bar Association and a Committee of Publishers and Associations.

In no way is it legal to reproduce, duplicate, or transmit any part of this document in either electronic means or in printed format. Recording of this publication is strictly prohibited and any storage of this document is not allowed unless with written permission from the publisher. All rights reserved.

The information provided herein is stated to be truthful and consistent, in that any liability, in terms of inattention or otherwise, by any usage or abuse of any policies, processes, or directions contained within is the solitary and utter responsibility of the recipient reader. Under no circumstances will any legal responsibility or blame be held against the publisher for any reparation, damages, or monetary loss due to the information herein, either directly or indirectly.

Respective authors own all copyrights not held by the publisher.

The information herein is offered for informational purposes solely, and is universal as so. The presentation of the information is without contract or any type of guarantee assurance.

The trademarks that are used are without any consent, and the publication of the trademark is without permission or backing by the trademark owner. All trademarks and brands within this book are for clarifying purposes only and are the owned by the owners themselves, not affiliated with this document.

CPSIA information can be obtained
at www.ICGtesting.com
Printed in the USA
LVOW10s0047050417
529648LV00007B/181/P